Professor E. H. Andrews
B.Sc., Ph.D., D.Sc., F.Inst.P., F.I.M.

FROM NOTHING TO NATURE

A young people's guide to evolution and creation

 EVANGELICAL PRESS

EVANGELICAL PRESS
P.O. Box 5, Welwyn, Hertfordshire AL6 9NU, England

© E. H. Andrews 1978
First published July 1978

ISBN 0 85234 120 2

Cover design Peter Wagstaff

*Printed in Great Britain by Robert MacLehose and Company Limited
Printers to the University of Glasgow*

FROM NOTHING
TO NATURE

To Rachel and Martyn

CONTENTS

INTRODUCTION

This book about creation and evolution has been written mainly for teenagers, therefore I have kept the language as simple as possible. Where technical words have had to be used, I have tried to explain them. To further help my younger readers I have used frequent word-pictures and verbal illustrations as well as forty diagrams and photographs.

Having said this, I should also say that I never under-estimate the intelligence of children and young adults! So I have not been afraid to use some quite deep arguments and to deal with some of the difficulties which are often glossed over in books of this kind. Because of this I believe that many adults will find the present work both interesting and rewarding to read. This will be particularly true for the many who have no scientific training and who thus find it difficult to follow writings on this theme which take for granted a certain knowledge of the technical background.

I have tried throughout to give an accurate, though simplified picture of what the theory of evolution really does teach. It is only when this is fully grasped that one can sensibly advance the many cogent arguments against Darwin's theory and the whole philosophy of evolution.

No doubt there will be some who read this book who do have a scientific education and who are, perhaps, convinced of the truth of evolution. I believe that even such readers will find much in these pages to give pause for thought. The arguments I have employed, though designed for young people and for those without significant scientific knowledge, are, I hope, sound. However, I have not always pursued those arguments in the depth that they may deserve. An example of this is the argument concerning chance and purpose in creation. To do justice to this subject would require us to discuss matters such as determinism in science, the nature of statistical processes and the way microscopical indeterminism leads to laws of macroscopic determinism. Such a discussion would have been out of place in this book, and I trust that my more sophisticated readers will understand this.

Finally, I would like to thank those who have encouraged the writing of this book, from the Reverend John Legg, who first suggested the project, to those young people who read and criticized the chapters as they were completed. Special thanks are due to my teenage daughter Rachel who not only read the manuscript but also suggested the title, "From Nothing to Nature".

EDGAR ANDREWS

WELWYN, *April* 1978

Chapter I

Where did we come from?

Made in God's image

Very young children often ask the question, "Mummy, where did I come from?" The mother may explain how babies are made and born and the child is satisfied with the answer. But what makes the child ask the question in the first place?

As soon as we are old enough to think, we begin to know that we are not just human beings but persons. Each of us knows that we have a self which is different from the self in our parents, brothers, sisters or friends. It is this self-knowing that makes us ask the question: "Where did I come from?" The child is not really asking where its body came from but rather where its self came from. The mother's reply is not an answer to that question.

The Bible teaches that the first man was made in the image of God. This means that Adam was given not only a body and a brain, but also a mind and a spirit. Animals have bodies just as wonderful and beautiful as our own. Animals, like us, have intelligence. They can learn and make their feelings known to us and to other animals. But only human beings have minds that can think and know their own selves. More than this, only human beings have a sense of right and wrong, which means they have a conscience. Lastly, the Bible says, humans have a god-like or spiritual nature which makes us quite different from even the most intelligent of our fellow creatures here on earth.

The Bible's answer to our question is that the self inside us is created by God. Like God Himself, we have minds, consciences and spirits. We are made in His image.

Later we shall see that God is at work all the time in everything that happens in this wonderful and mysterious world. He is at work in the making of our bodies. All the laws of science, which describe the way things happen within our own bodies and in the world around us, are controlled by God. So the Bible teaches. But when we say God creates us, ourselves, in His own image, we are saying even more than this. We are saying that God has made us not just part of His created world but part of His eternal kingdom. So man is a special creation of God, different from all the other creatures He has made.

Evolution

Today many people do not believe the Bible. Even people who believe in God often think the Bible is old-fashioned and mistaken when it describes the way that nature and man himself came into being. They say science has discovered that living things just happened by accident many millions of years ago. They believe that the first living thing was a very tiny, simple creature—perhaps like a virus. (Viruses give us illnesses such as colds and flu; a single virus particle is too small to see with the naked eye.) From this very simple creature, have arisen all the living things that exist today, or have ever existed, from fishes to fireflies, from eels to elephants and from mosses to maple trees. Finally, they say, there arose apes, monkeys and men. The whole thing took thousands of millions of years to happen.

This idea of how nature came to be is called the theory of evolution. "Evolution" means unfolding or developing. Although the idea of evolution was talked about by some of the thinkers of ancient Greece, over two thousand years ago, the modern theory of evolution was put forward by Charles Darwin in 1859. It is Darwin's theory, with some important changes, that is now taught in schools and on the radio and television. Most people in the western world believe it to be true.

The theory of evolution allows people to forget God. If mankind is just the result of millions of chance happenings, as the theory claims, there is no need to believe in a Creator: that is, a person we call God who made all things from nothing. Indeed, many people feel that if we can explain nature, including ourselves, by the idea of evolution, there is no need to believe in God at all! They say that God was just an idea needed in the old days to explain how the world was made. Now we have the theory of evolution, they argue, we no longer need God.

Of course, this is not true. Even if we accept the idea of evolution, it cannot explain everything. It cannot explain where the laws of science came from and it cannot explain how the world, the planets and the stars (which together we call the universe) came to exist in the first place. Evolution cannot explain such things as kindness, love, beauty, friendship and fairness. It cannot explain evil and good, nor can it help us to choose between them. Lastly, the theory of evolution cannot tell us where we are going when we die, except to say, "Nowhere". That is an answer we feel within ourselves to be wrong.

Because of this, many people try to believe in evolution and in God at the same time. There are many different ways of doing this. Some, for example, argue that God did make the worlds and everything in them but He used the chance happenings of evolution to do so. Just as a carpenter uses tools to make things out of wood, so God used the process (i.e. the workings) of evolution as a tool to create life and nature. Others say that evolution is still going on and that mankind will go on getting stronger and cleverer until we arrive at perfection. This perfect being will be God.

Still others imagine that God is not a person like ourselves but that nature is God or God is nature. Some of these ideas are difficult to follow. In fact they are more difficult to believe than the simple idea that a spirit, a person we call God, made us and that He continues to work in and through the universe to carry out His will and purpose.

Purpose or chance?

But why can we not believe in God *and* evolution? Many people will say we can, but I will tell you why I think that both cannot be true.

Firstly, the theory or idea of evolution teaches that all things happen by chance. I will be explaining in more detail in later chapters just what the theory does teach, and you will see that it supposes that everything happens by accident. There is no reason or purpose behind the universe. There is no guiding hand, no plan, in evolution. All that has happened in the past, including the rise of mankind, and all that will happen in the future are the result of blind chance.

When you throw a die, the number that comes uppermost does so by chance. Any one of six numbers is possible and if a three is thrown that is the result of pure chance. So it is with evolution.

Any one, not of six, but of thousands of possible changes might happen in an animal to help it evolve (i.e. change) into a slightly different creature. No one could guess what the final result would be, because, like the throw of a die, it is all settled by chance.

Let us imagine a game using a die. Suppose you decided to stand in the middle of a field with your die and a compass needle. Every time you throw the die you walk ten yards in some direction. If you throw a one, you walk north; if you throw a two you walk south. A three takes you east and a four leads you west. For a five or a six you do not move. Where will you be after a hundred throws of the die? There is no way of telling, because it is all governed by chance. You may finish up near your starting point or you may find yourself in one corner of the field. No one can tell.

So with evolution, no one can tell where it leads. If mankind is the best result of evolution, that is purely by accident or chance.

Creation by God is the exact opposite of this. It is not by chance or accident but because God planned to make nature and man. God meant to do it. He intended and wanted to create man. The Bible puts it very clearly: "Thou art worthy, O Lord, to receive glory and honour and power: for thou hast created all things, and for thy pleasure they are and were created" (Revelation 4: 11); "And God said: Let there be light and there was light" (Genesis 1: 3).

If God did really create all things, He did so because He wanted to and because He had a reason for making what He did.

If you are making a model out of wood or a dress out of cloth; if you are making a cake in the kitchen or building a hut in the garden, you are doing it for some good reason. You have some use or purpose for the thing you are making, otherwise you would not spend your time and effort on it! So God would not have made the worlds, nature or man without a reason.

How can we believe in God and His purpose and, at the same time, accept evolution and chance? Chance is the very opposite of purpose.

The Bible and evolution disagree

My second reason for not believing in God *and* evolution is that the Bible and evolution contradict each other. Of course some people do not think that matters. They say the Bible story of creation is a myth, rather like a fairy story. Some parts of the Bible, they say, are true but others are not. So they find it easy to believe in God and evolution at the same time.

But is it sensible to say that some parts of the Bible are true and that others are false? How do we decide which parts to believe and which parts not to? Is the Bible true when it tells us that Jesus Christ was God in human form but false when it says, "All things were made by Him"? Is the story of Abraham in the book of Genesis true (Jesus thought it was), but the story of creation in the same book untrue? Can we believe anything the Bible teaches about God if we accept that some parts of Scripture are fairy stories?

Jesus Christ obviously believed the Old Testament, including the story of creation. In fact He tells us that He came to fulfil (or keep) the many promises God had made in the Old Testament writings, including the book of Genesis. If Jesus Himself was wrong in believing the truth of these writings, how do we know His other teachings are right? What is left for us to believe?

Of course, there are other religions apart from the Christian faith. They have their own sacred writings and their own stories of how the world was made. But they face exactly the same problem with the theory of evolution because the very idea of a religion is that there is a meaning and a purpose in life. So the theory of evolution is in conflict with the holy writings of all religions.

If we say, then, that we believe in God *and* evolution we have the difficulty of deciding what kind of God we mean. Certainly He is not the God of the Bible who created all things by the word of His power. He is not the one described in the book of Psalms, who holds the breath of every living thing in His hands and controls life and death, seed-time and harvest, wind and rain. If we believe in evolution we are left with a God who, perhaps, started the world on its way but then left it to itself to struggle painfully upwards towards it knows not what. How different from the God described in the Bible who orders all things (in nature and among men) after the counsel (i.e. purpose) of His own will!

But someone may ask, "Does the Bible really contradict the theory of evolution? In what way do they disagree?"

Here are five important disagreements between Scripture and Darwin's theory.

THE BIBLE SAYS	EVOLUTION SAYS
Creation was planned for a purpose.	Nature evolved by accident and chance.
Living things were made separately, each one after its kind.	All living things came from a single life-form by evolution.
Man was a special creation, different from the animals.	Man is just another animal, evolved from ape-like creatures.
God's work of creation was finished in six days.	Evolution has continued to make new kinds of living things throughout time, and is still going on today.
Nature was created perfect but became spoiled because Adam disobeyed God.	Nature is always growing better and more perfect by evolutionary change.

These, then, are some of the reasons why I cannot believe in the theory of evolution *and* the Bible. They tell completely different stories and they cannot both be right!

Science and faith in God

So far I have given two reasons why I cannot believe in God and the theory of evolution at the same time. Now here is a third reason. This theory spoils the agreement or harmony between science and faith in God. All truth must be in harmony: that is, one true thing cannot contradict another true thing. They may be different truths but, in the end, they must agree with each other. Truth about God (we might call that spiritual truth) must agree with truth about nature (scientific truth).

It is very interesting that the men who started modern science and did the first scientific experiments and invented the first scientific theories were mostly people who believed the Bible. More than that, they believed that the new science would show others how wonderful is God's creation and so help them to worship God. One of the first and most famous of these scientists was Isaac Newton (1642–1727). He said very clearly that his science was intended to help people believe in God. Another was Robert Boyle (1627–1691) who wrote many books to show the harmony or agreement between the new science and the teachings of the Bible. Right up until 1859 when Charles Darwin put forward his theory of how life began and developed, most people found no conflict between science and the Bible.

Even today most of science shows how wonderful and mysterious is the world around us, and so agrees with the Bible. Science has no quarrel with the psalmist who said, "O Lord, how manifold (i.e. many) are thy works! In wisdom hast thou made them all: the earth is full of thy riches" (Psalm 104: 24).

Scientists are still discovering how beautifully the world is made, from the mighty stars to the tiny atom (see plate 1). As new things are discovered, new mysteries are also uncovered to give the scientists something new to think about and to explain. As the Bible says, God's works and wisdom are unsearchable: that is, they can never be fully explained. Only since the invention of very powerful microscopes, which can magnify millions of times, have scientists realised how complicated are the tiny living cells from which our whole bodies are made up. Each cell is no bigger than a speck of dust, yet inside it there is a whole factory, turning food into the thousands of different substances needed to keep our bodies in good health, alive and growing. Yet centuries ago the psalm-writer said of his own body, "I am fearfully and wonderfully made: marvellous are thy works" (Psalm 139: 14).

Science does not contradict the Bible, nor does the Bible contradict science. Science is another word for our knowledge of the world around us, and that knowledge, says the New Testament, ought to teach us certain things about God. St. Paul wrote, "The invisible things of God can be clearly seen in the world which He has created and understood from the things that He has made" (Romans 1: 20, paraphrased).

To many scientists this has been a true experience, for they have seen in the wonderful order and design in nature, the handiwork of God. When the famous astronomer, Johann Kepler, discovered how the planets move around the sun, he exclaimed, "O God, I am thinking thy thoughts after thee".

I do not mean that science can prove that God created the world, to someone who does not want to believe. We ought to recognize that nature is God's creation, but the Bible says we are like blind people who cannot see what is right in front of them. All the proof we need is there in the wonderful world around us, but we cannot see it because our minds are blind to spiritual truth (until God himself gives us the ability to see, but that is another subject). Science, then, cannot prove God. But neither does science contradict God. Even scientists who do not believe in God, or that He created the world, have to admit that the pattern and order, the beauty and the harmony of nature, are just as if there *had* been a great Maker who planned everything so perfectly.

This harmony or agreement between science and God is spoiled only by the theory of evolution. You must understand that science has hundreds, indeed thousands of theories. Each theory tries to explain certain facts of nature. The theory of gravity explains why things have weight and fall towards the ground. The same theory explains why the earth goes round the sun, and the moon around the earth. What we call the theory of electro-magnetism explains many things, including the way radio and television waves travel from the transmitter to your radio or television set. The theories of light or optics explain how lenses and cameras work and why a straight stick looks bent when you dip part of it under water. The list of theories goes on and on.

But only one theory, the theory of evolution, spoils the agreement between Bible truth and scientific truth. It is the only theory that does not fit into the great picture of truth.

Most of us enjoy doing jig-saw puzzles. As each new piece is fitted into the puzzle, the picture of the jig-saw becomes more clear. Our understanding of the universe is like a jig-saw puzzle. In the same picture there are scientific truths (truths about nature), and spiritual truths (truths about God). These different kinds of truth all help to make up the total picture of truth, just as different colours help to make up an actual jig-saw puzzle.

Even with all the truths shown to us about nature and God in the Bible, and the truths that science has discovered about nature, our picture is not complete. Lots of pieces are missing and we know only "in part" as St. Paul said long ago (I Corinthians 13 : 9), but the parts we *do* understand must all belong to the same picture!

Sometimes, though, when making jig-saw puzzles, a piece from one puzzle gets mixed up with the pieces from another. So when we do the puzzle we find a piece that doesn't fit and cannot fit because it is not part of the picture we are making. This odd piece has to be put aside because it does not belong. The theory of evolution is like that. To try to force it into the picture of truth can only damage the pieces already in place and can actually mislead us so that we cannot continue to build up that picture.

Evolution is not scientific

Now here is a fourth, and final reason why I do not think we can believe in evolution and the God of the Bible. This is to do with the theory itself. Scientifically speaking, evolution is not a good theory. It is a very weak theory because it is very difficult to test or prove. How can scientists find out whether a theory is a good one or not?

I expect you know something about motor cars or bicycles or clothes. These things and many others are familiar to us and, by experience, we learn to tell good from bad. If you are buying clothes you look carefully at the cloth they are made from. Is it good quality or not? Can it be washed without shrinking? You look to see if the stitching is neat and strong and whether the buttons are properly sewn on.

Fig. 1 It is wise to examine a second-hand car before buying it.

Buying a motor car, especially if it is not a new one, needs even greater care. You listen to the noise the engine makes and you test the steering and the brakes. You look to see if there is rust underneath the body-work. In short, you examine it carefully (see figure 1).

Scientists test a theory in just the same way. A theory is just an idea put forward to explain things that have been seen or observed. The theory of evolution is an idea put forward to explain the myriads of living things upon this earth. It is easy enough to think up a theory to explain certain things. It is much more difficult to know whether that explanation is right! So all theories have to be tested and examined, like the motor car someone is trying to sell you. You do not buy the car unless you are satisfied that it is a good one. Nor should we accept a theory unless we are sure it is a good theory.

In testing the car, we ask certain questions. Is the engine in good condition? Do the brakes work? Is the steering loose or worn? To test a scientific theory we also ask questions. They are questions like these.

Does the theory explain the facts?

Does the theory explain *all* the facts or just some of them?

Do any of the facts contradict the theory?

Can the theory be tested by doing special experiments, which will give a definite "Yes" or "No" answer as to whether it is right or wrong?

Is the theory precise or exact, or only vague?

When these tests and others like them are carried out on the theory of evolution, the theory does not pass them very well. It does not explain all the facts, and those that it does explain are not explained clearly. The theory does not show up well when tested by special experiments, because no experiment has yet shown evolution actually happening. (We shall discuss this in more detail in a later chapter.) The theory is often very vague and unclear, for example, when you ask exactly *how* one creature is supposed to have evolved or changed into another one. It is not able to give exact answers or even good guesses. Later we shall see more clearly some of the enormous gaps in the theory of evolution.

So evolution, the idea that all living things arose by chance from one, accidental life-form, does not stand up very well to the tests that scientists usually make to see whether a theory is a good one or a bad one.

Why, then, do scientists believe this theory? Well, of course, not *all* scientists do believe it, and the writer of this book is an example. But many scientists do believe in evolution for the same reason that many non-scientists believe it. They believe in evolution because they then do not have to believe in God. Many years ago Paul wrote of the wise men of his time, that they did not like to keep knowing God, and people are just the same today.

Chapter 2

What is life?

Different kinds of life

This book is about nature, the world of living things, and how it came into being. So it is important for us to ask the question: "What is life?" We cannot understand how something began without knowing what it is!

The question is easy to ask but difficult to answer. Although "life" is a word we use every day, the thing it describes is very wonderful and very mysterious. If people were really honest they would admit that none of us really understands what life is and how living things work.

The first thing to say is that there are different kinds of life.

A famous teacher once said, "I think, therefore I am". He did not mean, "I think, therefore I exist" because many things exist, including for example this book or the chair I am sitting on, which do not think. He meant, "I think, therefore I am alive". He, as a person, knew he had life because he was able to think. For him, his thoughts were the proof that he lived. This thought-life, the life of the mind, is one kind of life that we all experience.

But there are many living things that do not think. Plants, for example, are alive but they have no brain and cannot think thoughts as we do. How do we know that plants, such as flowers and trees, are alive? There are three things that show us.

Firstly, the plant can grow. It gets larger and makes leaves and flowers and fruit. The power to grow is one indication of life. Secondly, it responds to the things around it. Flowers turn to face the sunshine or the light; they sometimes close up at night and open again in the morning; they grow faster when it is warm and more slowly when it is cold. So the ability to respond or react to the surroundings is also evidence of life. Thirdly, and perhaps most important of all, the plant can reproduce. That is, one plant can produce or make other plants. It does this usually by growing seeds which, when planted in the earth, spring up as new plants exactly the same as the first or parent plant. The power to reproduce is a sign of life (see figure 2).

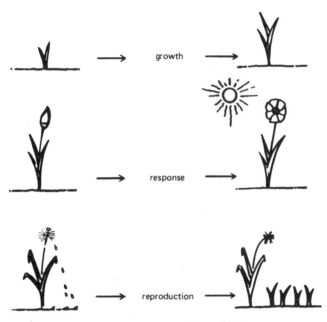

growth

response

reproduction

Fig. 2 The signs of physical life.

So you see we have already found two kinds of life. There is a kind of life which gives rise to thinking, and another kind of life which causes growth, response to the environment and reproduction. We shall need names for these different kinds of life in order to tell them apart. Let us call the thinking kind of life *mental life* because it tells us that there exists something we call mind. The life shown by growth, response and reproduction we shall call *physical life* because it is the kind of life shown by a body of some sort (whether of a plant, insect, animal or man). It is obvious that only a body can grow and reproduce and it is also obvious that all living creatures, including man, have this physical life. When physical life stops, we say the plant or animal is dead. Its body soon decays away until there is nothing left to see except, perhaps, a skeleton or shell.

Spiritual life

What I have said already shows there is nothing strange about the idea that there is more than one kind of life. As human beings we already know that we have two kinds of life, mental life and physical life.

Are there any other kinds of life? Yes, indeed. The most important kind of life, says the Bible, is spiritual life. It is the most important kind of life because it is the life of God.

God does not have a body. He is able to do all things and can therefore show (or manifest) Himself in a bodily way as He did in Jesus Christ. But God does not *need* a body as we do. God is a spirit. That means that He is not restricted to a body like we are. We cannot be in two places at once because our body keeps us in one of them! But God can be everywhere at the same time. No matter how fit and healthy we may be, our bodies get ill and finally must die. But a spirit lives for ever because it has no body to get sick or old.

So no spirit, not even God, has physical life. But the spirit is alive just the same. In fact, the Bible says that God has "life in Himself".This is another way of saying that God *is* life. As Jesus said, "I am the way, the truth and the *life*" (John 14: 6).

So the spirit we call God not only has life, but is life. He is the fountain of life from which all life (of all kinds, as we shall see later) comes. So we have to add a third kind of life. Let us set them out clearly to help us remember them.

Mental life   Physical life   Spiritual life
(living minds)   (living bodies)   (the life of God)

Because spiritual life is the life of God, and is therefore the most important (unlike mental and physical life, it cannot die), I am going to rearrange them so:

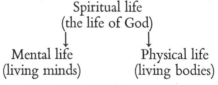

Spiritual life
(the life of God)

Mental life   Physical life
(living minds)   (living bodies)

We shall see later that spiritual life is not only the most important kind of life, but that all other kinds of life actually depend on the life of God. That is, there could be no other kinds of life without the life of God acting as a kind of foundation for it. Paul put it like this: "In him (i.e. in God) we live, and move, and have our being" (Acts 17: 28).

To explain a little more clearly what Paul was saying I am going to give you an illustration. Suppose you take a bowl of water and a dry sponge. The water is a picture of spiritual life and the sponge a picture of the physical world (see figure 3).

Fig. 3 A sponge in a bowl of water pictures the way the physical world is immersed in the spiritual world.

We could leave the sponge beside the bowl of water. There would be no connection, then, between the water and the sponge. They would be completely separate things. Some people think that spiritual life (and the spiritual world) is quite separate from physical life (and the physical world in which we live). Like the sponge and the water, they are both there but they are not connected or related in any way.

But this is not what the Bible teaches at all! Suppose you take the sponge and place it in the bowl of water. Now the sponge is not only surrounded by water but the water soaks all the way

through the sponge. The sponge is filled with water and surrounded by water. Both sponge and water are there, and we can
tell them apart, but they are now so close that the water goes all
the way through the sponge. If the water is clear we see only the
sponge just as before, but the invisible water is everywhere, around
the sponge and inside it.

This is just a picture of the way the invisible life of God flows
all through nature. This is what Paul means in the verse quoted
earlier, "In him (i.e. God) we live . . .". The hymn-writer meant
the same thing when he wrote,

"In all life Thou livest,
The true life of all".

Of course our picture is not a perfect one. According to the
Bible, the physical world only holds together because the spiritual
world is there. Physical life depends on the life of God and cannot
exist without it. For our illustration to show this, the sponge
would have to disappear if we took it out of the water and
squeezed it dry! Though this cannot happen with a real sponge,
perhaps we can imagine it happening and so make our picture
even closer to the things it is meant to illustrate.

When scientists study living things they cannot see the life of
God, but it is there just the same. We can use a microscope and
many other wonderful instruments to study physical life. The
tiniest molecules that make life work can be detected and studied
by science. But these ways of studying life can never see or find
the invisible spiritual world which is there, like the invisible water
in the sponge. To find that world we need, not a microscope, but
something called faith.

How does physical life work?

We now go back to look more closely at physical life. Later on, at
the end of this book, we shall say more about the connection
between physical life and spiritual life. We shall see how the Bible
explains the first in terms of the second. But for the moment we
are going to think about the kind of life shown by the growth,
response and reproduction of bodies, whether of plants or animals.

Science can tell us a great deal about physical life. The subject
we call biology is the study of life in its physical form. But many

other branches of science, like physics and chemistry, also have to be used to help us understand the wonders of physical life.

The Bible says that God created physical life and all living things. The theory of evolution says that physical life just happened accidentally. In the first chapter I explained why they cannot both be true, but before we can decide which is true, we need to know more about physical life. Exactly what is it and how does it work? In the rest of this chapter I will try to answer this difficult question.

Taking life to pieces

I wonder if you have ever taken a clock to pieces to find out how it works? If we want to find out how anything complicated works, the easiest way is to take it apart. So let us try to take to pieces a living body of some sort or other! It does not really matter what we choose to take apart because we shall find that all living things work in the same way! Perhaps this surprises you, but it is true.

Of course plants and animals are all very different. Squirrels have legs, and daisies have leaves; fish have scales and elephants have skin. What do I mean, then, when I say all physical life works the same way?

I mean that all living things are built up from tiny specks of living material called "cells". Mostly, these cells are too small to see with the naked eye, though some plant cells can be quite large, several millimeters in size. Just as a house is built up from many thousands of separate bricks, so living plants and creatures are made up of separate cells. Some tiny creatures are made up of just one cell, while others, like fish or mammals may contain countless millions of cells.

The same kind of bricks can be used to build many different looking houses. So an elephant and a worm are both made up of cells which, though different, are much more similar than are the two creatures themselves. Also, just as one house can be built from several different kinds of brick, so many different kinds of cell go to make up a single living plant or animal. There are different kinds of cell to make hair, skin, flesh, muscle, bones, blood, the liver and so on. But they can all be recognized as cells, each cell separated from its neighbours by the envelope or cell-wall that surrounds it.

In this chapter I am not going to talk about the way different cells are built up into different plants or animals. I am going to talk only about the cells themselves, because it is there, inside a single cell, that the real miracle of life is found.

If we take a house to pieces, we finish up with bricks—and a lot of other things, no doubt! But we cannot take a single brick to pieces, because it is the same material all the way through.

This is not true of a single cell. When, in our imagination, we have taken our elephant or our worm to pieces, and separated it into all its single cells, we have only just begun!

Most single cells are very, very complicated. Each cell is like a tiny factory! Like a factory, it is enclosed inside a wall and there are doors which let in some things (food and water for the cell) and let out other things (waste). But these doors are closed to anything that would harm the cell. Again, like a factory, there are machines inside the cell. These are tubes, films (or membranes) and tiny clumps of matter, in which the cell turns its food into useful chemicals. There are workers in this factory too! These are large molecules called "enzymes". (If you do not know what a molecule is, be patient. We are coming to that in a moment.) The enzymes actually make the chemical substances needed by the cell and by other parts of the body. There may be as many as fifty different kinds of enzyme in one cell, each making a different product.

But that is not all!

Somewhere in every cell is the nucleus.

The magic of the nucleus

The word "nucleus" means core or centre. In a living cell, the nucleus is a small mass of living material inside the cell which is kept separate from the rest of the cell's contents by its own envelope or membrane. In our picture of a factory, the nucleus is like a special office within the factory which is usually kept locked. Inside this office are kept the most important drawings and blueprints for the work of the factory.

In the picture (plate 2) you can see the nucleus in a cell very clearly. This picture was taken through an electron microscope which can magnify by more than a million times.

What is so special about the nucleus? There are two things.

Firstly, the nucleus of a living cell can divide itself into two new nuclei. When it does so, the rest of the cell follows its lead and also splits up into two parts, each having one of the new nuclei inside it. So, prompted by the nucleus, a single cell can become two cells, both exactly alike! This is how living things grow. One cell becomes two, two cells become four, four cells become eight and so on (see figure 4). In this way a tiny human egg cell, too small for us to see without a microscope, can grow into a baby, the baby into a child and the child into an adult. In exactly the same way a tiny apple pip can grow into a tree.

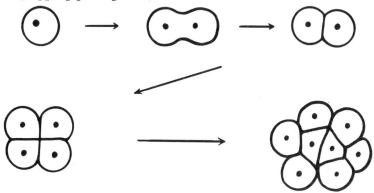

Fig. 4 Living cells multiply by dividing into two. The black dots represent the nuclei of the cells.

Although at first the cell splits into two exactly similar cells, there must come a stage in the growth of a living thing where the new cells are different from the parent cell. The cells are said to "differentiate", so that some become skin cells, others muscle cells, others bone cells, others blood cells and so on. But once these different kinds of cell have been formed, they go back to producing only cells of their own kind again! The magic of growth lies in the nucleus.

But there is a second reason why the nucleus is so important. Like the factory office I mentioned just now, the nucleus has inside it the plans or blue-print for the whole plant or animal! And every cell in the plant or creature contains the blue-print for the whole living thing!

Imagine that our factory, like the cell, is part of a large city of factories. The city represents the living thing (or organism) and each factory pictures one cell. There are many different kinds of factory in our city, each making different products, like the different kinds of cell in the organism—skin cells, bone cells, liver cells and so on. But in every factory, in a locked-up office, there are the plans and blue-prints for the whole city, not just that one factory. So if the whole city were burnt down and only one factory left standing, it would be possible to re-build the city exactly as it was before, using the information (i.e. the plans and blue-prints) found in that one factory.

Remember that we are still taking to pieces a living creature to find out how it works. We have found that all organisms are made up from cells. We have seen that each cell is made up from many parts, including the mysterious nucleus. Inside the nucleus are plans or blue-prints which tell us how the whole plant or creature is built. We now want to know what exactly are these plans or blue-prints. What are these instructions which tell the body how to grow and what to look like?

Once we know the answer to this question we will be as close as we can get to answering the question: "What is physical life?"

It is going to be quite difficult to explain the blue-prints or instructions which are held inside the cell nucleus. For this reason I am going to end this chapter here and give a whole new chapter to explaining this very wonderful matter. As I do so, I hope you will see how beautiful and complicated is the thing we call life. As we dig more deeply into the meaning of physical life we find that it gets more mysterious, not less.

The theory of evolution sometimes argues that small things, like single cells, are simple and that complicated things like the human body are built from these simple parts. We shall see in the next chapter, as we have done in this one, that small things like the cell and its contents are not simple. The flight of a bird and the running of the deer are very much easier to understand than the workings of a single cell!

Chapter 3

The secret code of life

Chromosomes and genes

I expect you have seen those gaily painted Russian dolls, carved out of wood, which open to reveal another, smaller doll, inside. When the smaller doll is opened, there is a still smaller one inside that, and so on. Taking apart a living organism is rather like opening these Russian dolls. Every time we look closely at a part of a creature or plant we find something smaller and more wonderful inside! I have to tell you that we have not yet finished finding smaller things inside.

We have pictured the living cell as a factory, and the nucleus as an office inside the factory. Let us now go into that office.

Imagine you walked into a room and found there a number of tall filing cabinets or cupboards. Each cabinet is filled with drawers from top to bottom. In each drawer there are many hundreds of sheets of paper, each with a different plan or blueprint on it (see figure 5).

This is just a picture of what is found in the cell nucleus. The tall cupboards represent small stick-like objects that can be seen, through a microscope, inside the nucleus just before it divides into two (see plate 3). Human cells have twenty-three pairs of these stick-like objects, but other organisms have different numbers. They are called "chromosomes" after the Greek words for colour and body. This is because they absorb the coloured stains used to show-up different parts of the cell under the microscope.

When the cell nucleus splits in half, one chromosome from each pair goes into each of the two new nuclei, so that each new cell exactly the same chromosomes. When the new cells are ready to divide, each of them doubles its chromosomes, making a pair out of each of the original ones, and the cycle is repeated.

If the cupboards represent chromosomes, what do the drawers represent? The answer is "genes". The genes are short lengths of the chromosome. As a pile of drawers make up a cupboard when fitted into a suitable frame, so the genes make up a chromosome when joined together. They are called genes because they contain the instructions needed to "generate" or make the animal or plant. One gene may control the colour of an animal's fur or the size of a flower's leaves. Another gene controls the colour of the eye. Others control the growth of all the complicated parts of a body, like the heart, lungs and brain.

Fig. 5   The filing cabinets picture chromosomes, the drawers picture genes and the plans picture DNA. There are, however, hundreds of genes in each chromosome, not just the few shown here.

But what are the genes made of? Inside the drawers of our cupboard, I said, there are hundreds of plans or blue-prints. And the genes are actually made up of long molecules of a substance called DNA. (Its full name is de-oxy-ribo-nucleic-acid, but let's call it DNA for short!)

The spiral staircase

A molecule is a group or cluster of atoms. Water has a very small molecule, H_2O, made up of two atoms of hydrogen (H) and one of oxygen (O). The molecule of DNA is a very large molecule made up of thousands of atoms arranged in a very special way. You can see how big the DNA molecule is by looking at figure 6 which shows a model of the molecule made up from balls; each ball represents one atom. DNA is made of atoms of carbon, hydrogen, oxygen, nitrogen and phosphorous, all arranged in a double helix or spiral.

This special arrangement is also shown in figure 6. The molecule of DNA looks just like a spiral staircase. The two sides of the staircase make the double spiral and the steps join the two spirals together.

There are just four different kinds of step, each made of different groups of atoms. Let us call these four different kinds of step A, B, C and D. Although just one DNA molecule has many thousands of steps in its spiral staircase, every step is either A, B, C or D.

It helps us to picture this if we imagine the different kinds of step to be differently coloured. Imagine you have four tins of paint, red, blue, green and yellow. You are asked to paint the steps on a tall spiral staircase. Any step can be painted red for A, blue for B, green for C or yellow for D. How many different ways could you paint the first ten steps?

Imagine some different ways. For example,
    red-blue-yellow-blue-green, etc.
or   blue-red-green-green-yellow, etc.
or   yellow-red-yellow-red-green, etc.

How many different ways?

You will be very surprised at the answer. There are more than a million different ways of painting the first ten steps of your staircase! The actual number is 1,048,576!

In the same way, a piece of DNA molecule, just ten steps long, can be built in more than a million different ways depending on the order in which the four steps A, B, C and D are placed. The number of different DNA molecules that can be built with a hundred steps is over a million millions. If there are a thousand steps, the number is a one followed by eighteen noughts!

Does this matter? Yes, it is very important. Because the exact

B

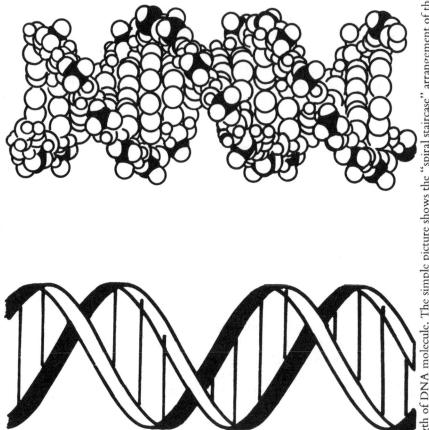

Fig. 6 A short length of DNA molecule. The simple picture shows the "spiral staircase" arrangement of the molecule. The complicated picture shows the atoms in the molecule. Each ball represents one atom. Black balls are phosphorous atoms and white balls are atoms of carbon, oxygen, nitrogen and hydrogen.

order of the steps A, B, C and D acts as a kind of code or a set of instructions.

Suppose you live in a street where all the houses look exactly alike. You cannot tell one house from the next one and none of the houses has a number or name. Suppose also that the front door of each house is reached by a short flight of steps going up from the pathway.

One way to tell the houses apart would be to paint the steps in different orders with our four colours. If each house has ten steps, we could paint the steps of more than a million houses without repeating the same order.

The order of the colours on the steps would then tell you which was your own house. It would also tell the postman or the milkman whose house it was. The order of colours would be acting as a code of instructions, telling everyone who knew the code which house is which.

In the same way, the order of the four steps in DNA works like a code giving instructions, not to the postman or the milkman, but to other molecules in the cell. That is why we have pictured the groups of steps in the DNA molecule as plans or blue-prints. As plans drawn on paper give instructions to a workman, so the steps in DNA give instructions to the cell.

So we have,

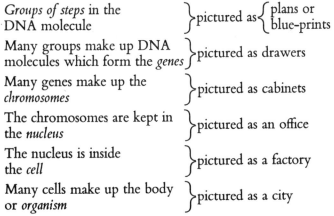

And the *kind* of body or organism depends entirely on those groups of steps in the DNA molecules, and the order in which those four different kinds of step are arranged.

Could this all have happened by chance? The theory of evolution says it did. But the Bible says that God designed it all. If an explorer came across a city in an unexplored jungle and found there factories and offices and plans, he would of course realise that it had all been designed on purpose by someone. He would not think it had happened by accident, because that would not make sense.

Yet evolution claims that the fantastic design and detail of living things (and especially the DNA molecule itself which carries the plans or blue-prints for all forms of life) *did* just happen by accident.

Let us see just how impossible this would be.

The code of life

The order of the steps in the DNA molecule makes up the code of life. Each group of steps along the molecule is like a plan or blue-print telling the cell how to make some substance needed by the body, or exactly how to grow. Let us look more closely at the code in which these instructions are given.

I imagine that most of us at some time or another have been interested in codes. We may have made up codes to carry secret messages between us and our friends that no one else could understand. An easy code can be made by letting the letter Z stand for the letter A, A for B, B for C and so on. Using this code, the word

ELEPHANT

becomes

DKDOGZMS

This is not a very good code because you need just as many letters in the code as you have in the original alphabet. So, although this code hides the meaning of words, it does not make our message more easy to pass on, and that is the chief purpose of a code. The morse code, in which each letter of the alphabet is replaced by a row of dots and dashes, is much better. In this code we need only two different bits of information, a dot and a dash. Any number of letters, words and sentences can be made up from groups of dots and dashes. This makes it *easy* to send messages or to transmit information.

Another example of a code is a telephone number. Using only ten different numbers, 0, 1, 2 and so on up to 9, we can tell the telephone machinery to connect us with any one of millions of telephones all over the world. By dialling 0202 1234 I can speak to someone in Bournemouth, but 0272 1234 connects me to a telephone in Bristol. By dialling more numbers in the right order I can speak to people in America, France or Germany. So by arranging only ten single figures (or digits) in different ways I can tell the telephone machinery to link my telephone to any one of millions of other telephones.

The reason why the telephone code works so well is easy to see. By arranging our ten digits in different orders, using each digit as many times as we like, we can make up an amazing number of four-figure groups, each of which is different. For example,

$$0121, \ 0122, \ 0123 \ \text{------}$$
$$0131, \ 0132, \ 0133 \ \text{------}$$
$$1130, \ 2130, \ 3130 \ \text{------}$$

In fact there are

$$10 \times 10 \times 10 \times 10 = 10,000$$

different four figure groups we can make up in this way. And there are

$$100,000 \text{ five-figure groups}$$
$$1,000,000 \text{ six-figure groups}$$
$$10,000,000 \text{ seven-figure groups}$$

and so on.

Now many telephone numbers (those in the United States of America, for example) have as many as ten digits. That means there are ten billion possible telephone numbers in the U.S.A.!

But there are not that many telephones! If there were ten billion telephones, every person in the U.S.A. would have fifty telephones!

Even if everyone had one telephone it would mean that only one ten-digit number out of every fifty possible numbers was a real telephone number. The other forty-nine possible numbers are meaningless and if you dial one of them nothing will happen.

What has this to do with the code of life?

Well, we have already seen that the four different kinds of step in the DNA molecule can be arranged in an enormous number of different ways. That is just like the ten digits being arranged in different ways to make possible telephone numbers.

But, like the telephone numbers, only a small fraction of the possible arrangements are actually found in DNA.

The way the DNA code works is this. The DNA molecule is like a template or pattern for the making of other molecules called "proteins". (Actually, another kind of nucleic acid called RNA is usually made first using the DNA as a pattern, and the proteins are then copied off the RNA—but the final result is the same.)

The proteins are long chain-like molecules built up from small units called "amino-acids". The DNA (or RNA) acts as a pattern making these small units link up in a particular order to make a particular protein. And it is the order of the steps in the DNA molecule that decides the kind of protein that is made. These proteins then control the growth and activity of the cell which, in turn, controls the growth and activity of the whole organism.

Now the point is this. Most of the possible chains of amino-acids do *not* make proteins found in living things. They make biological nonsense. Just as forty-nine out of every fifty *possible* telephone numbers in the U.S.A. are not real telephone numbers at all, so most of the possible chains of amino-acids are not real (i.e. biologically useful) proteins at all.

The "code of life" written on the DNA molecule makes sure that only the useful proteins are made.

It is not possible for a code, of any kind, to arise by chance or accident. The laws of chance or probability have been worked out by mathematics. These laws tell us that chance happenings would produce nearly all possible chains of amino-acids in equal amounts. There is no way that the few real proteins could be chosen out of all the possible ones simply by chance.

A code is the work of an intelligent mind. Even the cleverest dog or chimpanzee could not work out a code of any kind. It is obvious then that chance cannot do it.

The code of life exists because God thought it up and wrote it on the DNA molecules that control all forms of life. Using just one chemical substance, DNA, the Creator brought into being a multitude of different forms of life, simply by using a careful selection of the vast number of different messages that can be written using the code of life. As Paul says, "God giveth it (i.e. an organism) a body as it has pleased him, and to every seed its own body. All flesh is not the same . . . there is one flesh of men, another flesh of beasts, another of fishes, and another of birds" (I Corinthians 15: 38–39).

God, in creation, is like the composer who uses a single instrument like the piano, and a single code made up of the separate musical notes, to create a large number of different pieces of music. These may range from simple preludes to great piano concertos. So God has used a single substance, DNA, and a simple code of only four symbols, to create the vast range of living things, from the simplest virus to the wonder of a human brain.

This could no more have been the work of chance or accident than could the "Moonlight Sonata" be played by mice running up and down the keyboard of my piano!

Codes do not arise from chaos.

Chapter 4

How did life begin?

So far, we have seen a little of what life is, but really, we have only skimmed the surface. As we study in greater detail the world of living things, we discover more and more of its wonder, beauty and perfection. For example, we have talked about two kinds of molecules—nucleic acids and proteins—but there are many other molecules which are needed for living organisms to work. We have talked about the living cell, but many books have been written about the way cells are made and how they work. Science has answered many questions about physical life, but every answer leads to new questions. The more we discover about the secret of life, the more mysterious it is found to be.

We must now move on to another question. How did physical life begin? The Bible says that God created life and that He created the different kinds of living organism (plants, trees, fish, mammals, man and so on) "after their kind".

This can only mean that He created the different forms of life separately. According to the Bible, they did not all evolve from one original living cell, but were made, from the outset, as quite different creatures and organisms. The words "after their kind" also suggest that the forms of life created by God were, by and large, the forms of life we know today (plus, of course, those that have become extinct and which we only know from their fossils).

This does not mean that there have been no changes in the world of living things since creation. Living organisms were created with a great ability or capacity for change. God did this quite deliberately. If they were not able to change, creatures would not be able to adjust to changing conditions. The ability to change is one of the best forms of protection that an organism can have.

But the changes that have happened, and do happen even today, are within the kinds. Creatures do not change from one kind into another, no matter how long we wait. We must return to this subject in the next chapter, but in this chapter I want to consider what evolution teaches about the beginning, or origin, of life.

The idea of chemical evolution

Evolution and the Bible both agree that there was once no life on earth. The book of Genesis says, "The earth was without form and void (i.e. empty)" (Genesis 1: 2). They also agree that living things arose from the non-living material (or matter) of which the earth was made. Genesis declares that God formed both man and beast out of "the dust of the ground" and no doubt this was equally true of plants and trees. There is no suggestion in the Bible that life came from outside the earth, and most of those who teach evolution also agree that life began here.

Some scientists, though, seriously suggest that life was brought to earth from somewhere else in the universe, perhaps by meteorites. This rather strange idea was put forward to get round one of the great difficulties of the theory of evolution. This is that evolution needs thousands of millions of years to explain how life arose from non-living matter. Those who say life came from beyond the earth do not think the earth is old enough for life to have evolved here.

Most evolutionists, though, still believe that life began on earth. Please notice that they *think* it happened. They have no way of knowing that it *did* happen in the way they suggest.

Some people think that if we could find a way to create a living organism today, in a laboratory, this would prove that life began by the accidental joining-up of chemicals. They would say, "You see! If we mix these molecules together and use clever chemistry to link them up in just the right order, we get a living organism. So this is how life must have started!"

Well, for one thing, no one has yet been able to do this. It has been possible to take a virus particle apart, by separating its DNA from its protein, and then to put it together again so that it still works (i.e. can still infect living cells). Parts of other living things have also been taken apart chemically and then put together again. But so far no one has been able to make a living thing out of non-living molecules, try as they may.

But even if they did, it would not prove that this is what happened, by accident, when life first appeared on earth.

In fact it would prove something quite different! It would show that the creation of life out of non-life needs skill, knowledge and intelligence. For unless the scientist had these it is certain that his experiments would fail. It is not enough to take simple, non-living molecules, mix them together and expect a living molecule to emerge. If life is ever going to be made in a test-tube we know it will be because a highly skilled scientist controls the way the simple molecules join together or react. It will be the scientist's intelligence that stamps the code of life on his material.

In the same way the Bible teaches that God formed living things out of non-living matter (or dust) from which the earth is made. It was God's intelligence, knowledge and infinite skill that did then what scientists (copying His blue-print) may one day be able to do themselves.

But let us come back to what evolution teaches on this subject. The idea of chemical evolution is that ordinary chemical substances joined together (or combined) to make the first living molecule, i.e. a molecule like DNA which was able to reproduce itself. This idea is based on two simple facts. Firstly, living molecules, like DNA and proteins, are made up of exactly the same atoms as are non-living molecules. They contain atoms of oxygen, hydrogen, carbon, sulphur and so on which are just the same atoms as are found in water, marsh gas and other simple substances. There are no atoms in living molecules that are not found in non-living ones. Living molecules are different only because of the way their atoms are put together and because, normally, they can only be made by living organisms. This, of course, is exactly what the Bible means when it says that God "formed" living things out of "the dust of the ground". In fact, considering that Moses knew very little chemistry, this statement in Genesis is really rather remarkable! It would be much more natural to think that living and non-living things are made of completely different materials.

The second simple fact is that, under the right conditions, small molecules can be made to combine to form larger, more complicated molecules. The whole plastics industry is based on this fact. For example, polyethylene, a common plastic, is made by joining thousands of small ethylene molecules into a single gigantic chain (see figure 7).

So, say evolutionists, it is quite possible that small molecules like methane (CH_4), water (H_2O), ammonia (NH_3) and hydrogen

(H_2) joined together to make larger molecules and that these again combined to make a molecule that could begin to live.

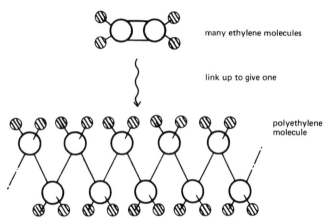

many ethylene molecules

link up to give one

polyethylene
molecule

Fig. 7 Ethylene gas molecules can be joined together to make a common plastic, polyethylene.

The early atmosphere

The small molecules, mentioned above, may have been present in the air or atmosphere of the earth when it was first formed. Now, of course, our air is made up almost entirely of nitrogen and oxygen, with small amounts of carbon dioxide and other gases. It is fairly certain that if the early earth had oxygen in its atmosphere as it has today, life could not have evolved by chemistry. This is because oxygen breaks down big molecules into smaller ones, and would have destroyed large molecules long before they reached the stage of living.

So the evolutionist says that the early earth did not have oxygen in its atmosphere, but only gases that would not harm the large evolving molecules. They say that all our oxygen must have been made by green plants which produce oxygen by a natural process called photosynthesis. This may, of course, be correct. It may equally well not be correct. There is no scientific proof either way. Certainly there always has been plenty of oxygen on earth, because the rocks contain vast amounts of it. Whether there was free oxygen, as there is today, we just do not know.

But oxygen poses some difficult questions for evolution. Today nearly all forms of life depend on oxygen. Without it they could not survive. But the earliest forms of life could not have needed oxygen (if evolution is right), because there was no oxygen for them to breathe. In fact oxygen would probably be poisonous to such living things.

So we have to believe that, at some point in time, organisms which could not live in oxygen changed (perhaps gradually) into organisms that could not live without it!

This may be possible, but it seems rather unlikely! It also means of course, that we can really have no idea what these early forms of life were like. They would have been very different from living things today, which depend on oxygen for life. (There are a few organisms, such as some bacteria, which do not need oxygen, but no one suggests that these are the early forms of life imagined by the evolution theory.)

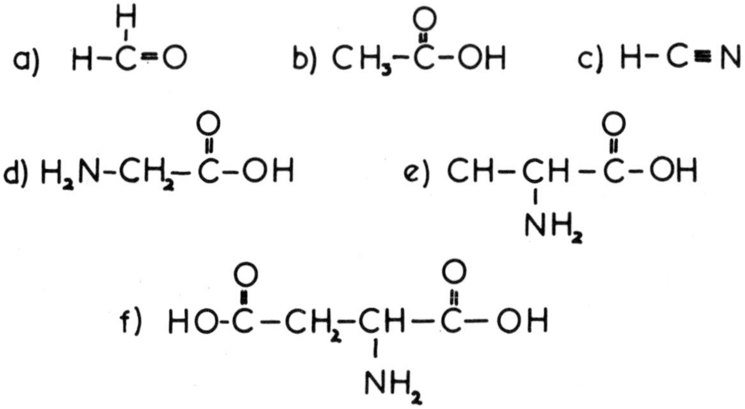

a) H–C=O   b) CH₃–C–OH   c) H–C≡N

d) H₂N-CH₂–C–OH   e) CH–CH–C–OH
                                              NH₂

f) HO-C–CH₂–CH–C–OH
                    NH₂

Fig. 8 Some of the molecules that can be made by passing a spark through a mixture of simple gases: (a) formaldehyde; (b) acetic acid; (c) hydrogen cyanide; (d) glycine; (e) alanine; (f) aspartic acid.

The sun, the lightning and the soup

This heading is not meant to be funny! Evolution teaches that the first step in joining small molecules to make larger ones took place in the sky. Either lightning or the sun's rays made molecules of methane, water, ammonia and carbon dioxide join up to make large organic molecules. (An organic molecule is one containing carbon.)

Now, it is quite true that an electrical spark (or discharge) can make these small molecules join up to make larger ones. This experiment has been done many times in the laboratory. The same kind of thing happens if ultra-violet light is used instead of a spark. (Ultra-violet light is what causes sunburn.) Even passing small molecules over heated sand will produce small amounts of large organic molecules. Some of the molecules that can be made in these ways are shown in figure 8. We must remember that although these new molecules are larger than the ones we started with, they are still very small compared with the molecules of life, like proteins and nucleic acids.

If these new molecules had stayed around in the sky they would soon have been broken down again by the same energy that made them in the first place, by ultra-violet light from the sun, for example. So, it is said, they must have been washed down by rain to the earth where they collected in the rivers, ponds and seas (see figure 9).

Over millions of years, says the theory of chemical evolution, more and more organic molecules were added to the waters on earth until they formed a "soup" or concentrated mixture of organic molecules and water. This soup might have become very thick, or concentrated, in pools left by the tide and which dried out partly in the sun.

Let us be quite clear that there is no proof at all that such a soup ever existed. It is something that *might* have happened if all the conditions were just right. Later on, the same theory uses the idea that the organic molecules would not mix very well with water (just as oil and water do not mix). But for the soup to be formed at all, and to remain the same for millions of years, the organic molecules must have mixed well enough with water to be carried down by raindrops and not lost as the water ran over the rocks and filtered through the ground. Like the earlier argument about oxygen we see that the theory likes to have it both ways; the molecules mix with water when it suits the theory but separate from water when that suits the theory too.

To be fair, what the theory claims is not impossible. Many substances will mix with water in small amounts but will separate, as oil separates from water, if the amounts are larger. Nevertheless, the theory of evolution always assumes that the conditions are just right, and this is not a very scientific way of thinking. To get over this difficulty the theory falls back on the argument that anything will happen, no matter how unlikely it is, if you allow

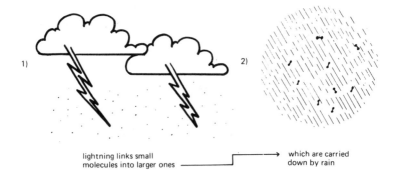

1)

lightning links small
molecules into larger ones

2)

which are carried
down by rain

3)

and collect in pools

4)

5)

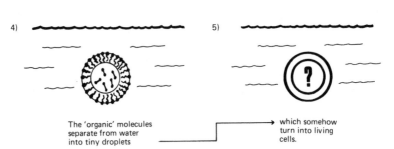

The 'organic' molecules
separate from water
into tiny droplets

which somehow
turn into living
cells.

Fig. 9 The origin of life according to chemical evolution.

enough time. That is why evolution always talks about millions and millions of years.

The final steps to life?

Two further steps are supposed to have happened before life was formed. Firstly the organic molecules in the concentrated "soup" are supposed to have begun to join together like links in a chain to form the really large molecules found in living things. I cannot explain here the very complicated chemistry involved in this linking together but there are three things that must have been just right if it really did happen.

Firstly, of course, the right molecules must have been present in the soup, and they must have been there in the right amounts. Secondly, the linking-up to make very large molecules like proteins and DNA cannot happen if there is water around, unless there are some very special molecules called "catalysts" to work against the effect of the water. Once again, it is not impossible that these special molecules were there, just at the right time and in the right amounts. It is not impossible that they were available and not taken up with other uses. Nothing is impossible, but it is all very unlikely. It is interesting that, even using these catalysts, no one has yet been able to join together more than just a very short length of protein-like or DNA-like chains.

Thirdly comes the greatest difficulty of all. How did the organic molecules link up in the special order needed for living molecules? For example, we saw in the last chapter that the amino-acids have to link together in rather special ways to make real proteins. Any old order will not do, yet in a mixture of amino-acids the linking-up would be nearly random. Again, we have seen that the order of the units in DNA is very important, but there is no chemical reason why the order should be of one kind rather than another.

The evolutionist really has no answer to this problem of order. Some suggest that minerals, like clay, which have an ordered crystal structure might have acted as patterns making the molecules link together in some ways rather than others. But this really is difficult to imagine. The crystals of clay have a very simple pattern. They do not contain enough information to tell amino-acids how to link up into a protein, or to stamp the code of life on a growing DNA molecule. It is like asking you to write an essay on biology using only words of two or three letters; it would

be impossible to do because such short words do not contain
enough information.

I said there were two further steps before life could arise from
the organic soup. The first step was the growth of giant, ordered
molecules from the ingredients of the soup, and we have just been
thinking about that. Now we come to the second step, which is
the forming of the first living cell.

You see, single molecules even of protein or DNA are not
living creatures. Even these molecules of life have to be arranged
(or organised) into one or more cells. It is true that virus particles
are made only of DNA molecules with a coating of protein. But
viruses are not really alive. They can only live and multiply when
they are inside living cells. All real forms of life are composed of
cells, though some creatures have just a single cell. Nevertheless
we do not know of anything that truly lives which is not made up
of one or more cells.

So evolution must not only explain how the molecules of life
were formed but also how they came together to make a cell.
Here are some of the ideas put up to explain how the first cells
were formed, entirely by accident, of course!

Evolution suggests that as the soup became concentrated, the
organic molecules began to separate from the water much as oil
drops separate from water after oil and water are shaken up
together. Some molecules, like those of soap or detergent, have
one end which mixes with water and the other end which mixes
with oily liquids. If such molecules were present they would have
collected at the surface of the oily droplets to form a kind of skin
(or membrane) around the droplet. Some other molecules may
have attached themselves to the inside of this skin, making a
double-layer like the membranes found around and inside living
cells (see figure 9, page 36).

That is as far as evolution can explain the forming of a living
cell. But a droplet of organic molecules, even with a double membrane around it, is as different from a living cell as a pile of bricks
is different from a factory in full working order. We have seen
how complicated and organised is a living cell. It is like a well-
managed factory with buildings, machines, production lines,
workers, offices and blue-prints. The drop of oil which, evolution
says, turned into a living cell is, at best, no more than an empty
building in comparison.

As usual, of course, the evolutionist waves his hands and explains that there were many millions of years for the droplet to turn into a living cell. But, of course, this is nonsense. Neither oil drops nor living cells last for very long! Oil drops will join together and float to the surface of the water with which they have been mixed, to form a separate layer. Even if we take great care to make an oil and water mixture (called an emulsion), so that it will last, it cannot do so for ever. Emulsion paint is spoiled if it is allowed to freeze, for example. Living cells, even in a living body, are always dying and being replaced by new ones. How, then, can we believe that organic droplets, or any half-way stage between the droplet and a living cell, lasted for the millions of years it might have needed for the cell to be produced? And if it did not need so many years, why cannot a living cell be made today in the laboratory by mixing the right molecules together and waiting for them to arrange themselves into a cell?

A story you will not believe

You may have found this chapter rather hard work so far. So I am going to give you some light relief by telling you an unlikely story. You will see the point of it in a moment.

One day I was walking along the sea shore when I saw something colourful half buried in the sand. Prodding it with my foot I saw that it was one of those small, solid rubber balls that bounce so well. How did it get there?

You may think that a child, playing on the beach the day before, had lost it, but I am going to give you a quite different explanation.

Many hundreds of years ago, on a tropical island, there grew, side by side, a coconut palm and a rubber tree. One day a coconut fell from the top of the palm tree to the ground, striking a stone which chipped off a small piece of the coconut shell.

It was not long before the ants and other insects found the hole in the coconut and began to nibble away the inside of the nut, till eventually the hollow shell was left quite clean inside.

It so happened, about that time, that a second nut fell from the palm tree. In falling it struck one of the main branches of the rubber tree, breaking off a piece of bark. Naturally, the milky rubber latex began to flow from the damaged branch and drip to the ground.

It so happened (I said that before, didn't I?) that the empty coconut shell lay directly below the damaged limb, with the small hole in its shell facing upwards. By a wonderful coincidence the rubber latex began to drip directly into the hole until quite a pool of latex had collected in the shell.

Then a wind sprang up, carrying sand and dust across the island. Some of the dust was mineral sulphur and some was from red-coloured rocks on the island. The wind piled the dust against the coconut shell and quite a lot of dust found its way into the hole and settled on the rubber latex.

Finally, the wind brought a leaf, which settled over the hole and latex drips then sealed this across the hole so that nothing could get in or out. The sea, driven by the wind, surged over the beach and swept the coconut shell away.

As the shell bobbed up and down, tumbling over and over in the waves the rubber latex mixed with the sulphur and the sand and rolled itself into a ball. Now when sulphur is heated with rubber it vulcanizes the rubber into a solid, elastic lump and this was just what happened now. (We have to imagine a hot sun, but that poses no problems!) The latex continued to be rolled around inside the much larger coconut shell while it was being vulcanized, and so took on a perfectly round shape. The coloured dust streaked the now-elastic ball with bands of red and yellow.

Eventually, the coconut was dashed against some rocks and broke, releasing the ball which floated and was finally thrown up on a beach where I found it.

Do you believe my story? No? Tell me why you do not believe it. I expect you would answer that it is all very unlikely. You cannot say it is impossible because I have taken great care that every step in my explanation is perfectly possible! Nothing I have said is scientifically impossible, and some of the ideas I have used are based on processes well known to science.

What fault can you find, then, with my story? You say it is unlikely, and you are correct. I have taken a series of happenings, each of which is perfectly possible but rather unlikely, and I have joined them together to explain how the ball came to be on the beach. If you say that the chance of all of these unlikely events happening, one after the other, is very, very small, I will simply reply that there was a very long time for it to happen. If you say it couldn't happen even in hundreds of years, I will reply, "All right. It may have taken thousands of years for everything to come just right!"

I think you will give up trying to prove me wrong, but you will still be quite sure that the rubber ball did not just "happen" the way I said it did.

The point of the story

The theory of chemical evolution is very like my explanation of the rubber ball. None of the steps in the theory can be proved to be impossible. Many are unlikely, but that difficulty is turned aside by saying that even the most unlikely things will happen if you wait long enough. Perhaps the rubber-ball story will make you question this idea that anything that is possible must happen if you give it enough time. This is an idea which comes up time and time again in the theory of evolution and it is wholly false. It is based on a misunderstanding of what we call "probability theory".

In the rubber-ball story, I strung together about ten different unlikely happenings, every one of which had to happen at just the right time to get the final result. So it is with evolution's story of how life began.

The early atmosphere had to contain some small molecules and not others.

Lightning or ultra-violet light had to be present to make them link together, but not to break them down again.

The new, larger molecules had to be washed down by rain. The molecules had to be below the clouds for this to happen, but the small ammonia molecules which dissolve very easily in water, were somehow *not* washed out of the sky. (This is hard to believe, is it not?)

The larger molecules, though not very soluble in water, had to stay in the water as it filtered through the soil and ran over the rocks.

These molecules, though lighter than water, had to remain under the water. If they floated to the surface they would have been destroyed by ultra-violet light.

The molecules had to collect and become concentrated in the organic soup so that they could be made to link together.

There had to be some very special catalyst molecules to make the organic molecules link up in water.

The right organic molecules had to be present in the right amounts to link up into proteins and DNA.

Somehow, the special coded order of proteins and DNA had to happen. No convincing or even possible explanation for this has yet been given.

Organic droplets had to form and stay around long enough for something to happen inside them which would turn them into living cells. No one knows how this something could have happened.

Finally, of course, the first living cell had to find out how to divide into two before it died (single cell animals do not live very long lives, especially in strong solutions of ammonia which we use to kill germs today).

Here we have eleven steps, each of which had to be just right for life to survive. None of the steps, separately, is completely impossible, though we have no idea how one or two of them could have happened. But strung together to give an explanation of the origin of life, they add up to a very unlikely story!

And that brings us back to the rubber ball. I wonder which you find more convincing, the story of the rubber ball, or the theory of chemical evolution?

Chapter 5

Darwin's theory

Two simple ideas

Did all the thousands of different plants, animals and insects we know today evolve from just one living cell which came into being by accident? This is what Darwin's theory of evolution teaches. We have already seen that this idea contradicts the Bible's story of creation. In the last chapter we also saw that it is very unlikely that the first living cell just happened by accident.

When Darwin wrote his book *On the Origin of Species* in 1859, he knew nothing about the theory of chemical evolution which we looked at in Chapter 4. His own theory took it for granted that some kind of life had been created or had come into being in some other way. Darwin's idea of evolution starts where chemical evolution finishes.

In this chapter we are going to think about Darwin's ideas. What is taught today is called "neo-Darwinism" which simply means the "new" theory of Darwin, i.e. Darwin's ideas brought up-to-date. We shall see what neo-Darwinism teaches and whether it is really as scientific and convincing as most people think.

The theory is based on two very simple ideas. The first is that living things can change or vary. The offspring or children of an animal or plant are often different in some way from their parents and from one another. Some offspring are stronger than others. There may be colour differences, blue eyes and brown eyes, for example, or differently coloured fur. Some are large and others small. These differences between organisms of the same kind we call "variations".

The second idea is "natural selection" which means choice by nature. Sometimes we call this "the survival of the fittest" because it means that the creature that copes best with its surroundings is less likely to die. It is more fit, or able, to stay alive and have its own offspring.

These two ideas are joined together to explain evolution. This is how it is supposed to work.

The story of the rapid rabbit

Imagine that five baby rabbits are born to the same parents. The babies are all a little different from one another and one of them grows up to be a very fast runner. He is always able to beat his brothers and sisters in a race.

So variation between the rabbits has given an advantage to this particular rabbit; he can run away from danger faster than the rest of his family. Let us call him the Rapid Rabbit.

Now suppose a fox visits the field where the rabbits live, to hunt for prey. He comes night after night and catches a rabbit each time. Perhaps he catches three out of the family of five but he cannot catch Rapid Rabbit (figure 10). By luck one of the other rabbits also survives.

Now only two rabbits are left but they find mates and each has

Fig. 10   Natural selection at work.

five baby rabbits of his own. Rapid Rabbit's family take after their father and are all good at running. The other rabbit's children are just ordinary rabbits.

Soon the fox returns and begins to hunt again. The family of Rapid Rabbits always escape because they can reach their holes before the fox catches up with them. The other family is not so lucky and soon only one is left alive. So when the parents die, there are five Rapid Rabbits left but only one ordinary rabbit! Most of the rabbits are now good runners, though the first Rapid Rabbit was only one out of five in his generation.

Natural selection or the survival of the fittest has made sure that a group (or population) of ordinary rabbits become mostly Rapid Rabbits in just two generations. So the rabbit population has become better able to escape from its enemies. It has changed for the better. It has moved a little way along the pathway of evolution.

This all seems very convincing, doesn't it? And up to a point, of

course, it is quite true. Populations or groups of animals or plants can and do adapt themselves to the dangers that they face. If they did not, they would not last very long.

But this does not mean that rabbits can turn into hares! The rabbits may become very fast runners. They may get better at escaping from their enemies. As generation follows generation they may also develop better hearing and a better sense of smell, so that foxes cannot creep up on them unnoticed. But they are still rabbits. They may be super-rabbits, but rabbits they remain!

Evolution teaches the opposite of this. It says that the changes we have talked about go on happening so that, little by little, the rabbit may turn into a new kind of animal—perhaps a hare, which has strong back legs and runs faster than any rabbit.

Evolution's map and compass

So evolution is supposed to work, firstly, by variation. We shall see later how variations come about, but for the moment we accept that offspring are different, in small ways, from their parents. But variation alone cannot cause evolution. Natural selection is needed to guide or direct the changes that take place from one generation to the next.

Imagine that a walker is taken by helicopter to some remote mountain country and told to find his way back to civilisation. There are no roads, no signposts and no one to ask the way. Our hiker will set off in some direction, but as night falls he is likely to lose his way. After walking for several days he may well find himself back where he started. (We will suppose the sun is hidden by cloud so that he cannot get his bearings from that.)

Variation among animals and plants is like our traveller's journey. It goes in any direction, quite by chance, and is likely to go round in circles, always returning to the place where it started. This is not evolution. Evolution is like a road that leads away from the starting point and reaches to some other place or destination. The road may wind and fork, but it always leads onward away from its starting place.

The problems of our traveller would be completely solved if we gave him a map and compass. Now he could find out where he is and set a course for the place he wants to reach. He may not be able to go in a straight line but he will always be making progress in the direction he wants to travel.

Natural selection is supposed to be the map and compass of evolution. By choosing some variations as favourable and rejecting others as harmful, natural selection guides the chance process of variation. So instead of going round in circles, the changes in plants and animals add up, like the traveller's steps, to a journey of progress, i.e. of evolution. That, at least, is the theory.

Let us see what sort of a guide natural selection really is.

Natural selection falls down

In fact there are three good reasons why natural selection cannot cause evolution. First of all, natural selection makes a group of animals more alike than they were to start with.

Think of our rabbits again. Suppose the fox and other enemies kill all the slow rabbits, all the rabbits who cannot see or hear very well and all the rabbits whose fur does not give them good camouflage. What are left? The rabbits that stay alive and breed will be those which are strong, sharp-eared and keen-eyed, and which have brown fur to hide them against the soil. They will all be like one another because the rabbits which are different will be caught and killed. So natural selection makes a group of animals more alike, not more varied.

But evolution says that at the start one life form became two different kinds of creature; those then evolved into several more different kinds and so on. Evolution says that groups of plants and animals grow more and more different until two different kinds arise from one original kind. If this is true, it cannot have happened by natural selection, because natural selection makes creatures more alike not more different. Natural selection works in the opposite direction to evolution.

Evolutionists try to get round this problem by saying that a group of animals or plants might get separated into two groups. If the two groups then live in different surroundings, natural selection will work differently on the two groups and make them more and more different. Although this may happen sometimes, it is very difficult to imagine it happening often enough to explain the whole of evolution, from amoeba to man. Also, the different surroundings of the two groups would have to be very different for this to have much effect. Yet even today mice in Africa are not very different from mice in Greenland, which shows that large

differences in food and climate, for example, support similar
animals equally well.

The second reason why natural selection cannot cause evolution
is that it could never bring about all the changes needed at the
same time to turn one kind of animal into another.

You might imagine that the hare evolved from a rabbit because
a hare looks like a rabbit which has just grown long legs. But a
zoologist will tell you that there are many hidden differences
between rabbits and hares. The proteins in their blood, for
example, are quite different and so are many other of the important body chemicals. Using this same bio-chemical argument you
can also show that, in some ways, man is more closely related to
pigs than to monkeys, and so on. Just because one animal (or plant)
looks rather like another does not prove that one has evolved from
the other, or even that they have evolved from a common ancestor.

There are so many differences, even between very similar
animals, that natural selection cannot explain all the changes that
would have to happen at the same time to turn one into another.
This is still true even if we allow that natural selection happens
through many different causes (enemies, food supply, the climate
and so on).

We now look at the third reason why natural selection falls
down as a cause of evolution. We shall see in a moment that the
variations between parents and children are small ones. Evolution
is supposed to happen by millions of small changes. To evolve a
complicated organ like the eye (see plate 4), or even simple things
like skin or hair, would need a very, very large number of such
small changes in the genes of an animal. Now it is obvious that a
creature with an eye has advantages over a similar creature without
an eye. But what advantage has a creature which has evolved only
part of an eye? If the lens of the eye had evolved, but not the light-
sensitive "retina", the creature would be just as blind as it was
before. Even if the whole eye had evolved, bit by bit, the animal
would still be blind until the optic nerve and brain cells had also
evolved.

The step-by-step evolution of organs is supposed to happen
because each step is favoured by natural selection. But natural
selection can only work in this way if each step gives the creature
some advantage. Obviously, hundreds of steps would have to
happen before any advantage was got from the evolving eye,

and these steps could not therefore be guided by natural selection.

Think again of our hiker in the mountains. Without a map and compass he will go round in circles. We have seen that natural selection is supposed to show evolution the way to go. But natural selection cannot begin to help with the evolution of the eye until the new organ begins to give some advantage.

This is like telling our traveller that there *is* a map and compass but that they have been left some miles away at a certain spot. If he can find his own way to that place, he can have the map and compass for the rest of his journey!

But how will he find that place without the help of the map? How will he know what direction to take without the compass? We have set him an impossible task.

It is just as impossible for something like the eye to evolve by natural selection; too much of the journey towards the finished eye would have to be done before natural selection could begin to help.

By the same argument it is impossible to imagine how the heart, the lungs, the liver and all the other important parts of an animal could have evolved by natural selection. Only the most simple organs could develop by the workings of natural selection and even then it is difficult to see how.

More about variation

The idea of variation among living things does not contradict anything taught in the Bible. The man who wrote the book of Genesis, Moses, had married an Ethiopian woman. He knew that some human beings have white skins and some black. He knew that there were different races among mankind. He may never have met a pygmy but he certainly knew there were giant humans, and wrote about them! Yet he explains that all humans came from Adam, and that God created one man and not several different kinds of men. All the differences or variations among humans must have arisen during the lifetime of the human race. That is quite clearly the teaching of the Bible (see figure 11).

In the same way many changes must have taken place in the plant and animal kingdoms. If black men and white men, pygmies and giants, could all come from one man, Adam, then several different sorts of thrush, or earthworm, may have arisen from single pairs of parents. The Bible does not deny that variation happens among animals and plants.

But the Bible does say that God created different "kinds" of animals, trees and plants at the start. They did not all come from a single life-form. The different kinds were created separately and did not change from one kind into another kind.

We do not know exactly what were the kinds. Did God create lions, tigers, panthers and leopards as separate kinds? Or have they all arisen from a single "kind" by variation, as the different human races arose from one man, Adam? We do not know.

One idea is that the kinds in Genesis were the same as "species" today. A species is a group of living things which normally breed only within their own group. So a particular species of bird or moth will not breed with other birds or moths, even though the other creatures may be rather similar to them.

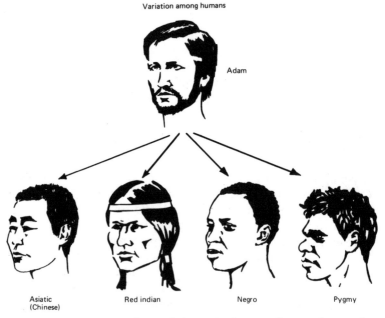

Variation among humans

Adam

Asiatic   Red indian   Negro   Pygmy
(Chinese)

Fig. 11   Variation among human beings. We do not, of course, know what Adam looked like!

If the kinds in Genesis are the species we know today, then lions and tigers would have been different kinds from the outset. But it *is* possible to mate a lion with a tiger to give an animal sometimes called a "liger"! And biologists do not always agree on what a species is, especially in the case of very simple organisms like bacteria.

So it is probably safer not to think of the kinds mentioned in Genesis as being exactly the same as species today. What is clear from Genesis is that God created many different kinds of plant, many different kinds of fruit tree, many different kinds of fish, many different kinds of bird and so on. He did not make one tree from which all others came or a single bird which gave rise to all the different sorts of birds we know today. Certainly He did not create one creature which then evolved into all the forms of life which ever lived.

How does variation happen?

We have seen that variation happens within the kinds that God created in the beginning. We have seen how black men and white men all descended from a single man and woman. It is also clear that quite large variations happen within groups of animals and plants. Just think how many different varieties of dogs there are! I have no doubt that all dogs came from just one original pair and similar animals, like wolves and foxes, probably also belong to the same created kind as dogs.

But how do variations come about? It can happen in three quite different ways. In organisms which breed by mating, the egg cell from the mother and the seed cell from the father each has only half the number of chromosomes found in other cells. All human cells have 46 chromosomes except the egg and seed cells which have only 23 each.

So when the egg and seed join together the resulting cell has the full number of chromosomes. It is this fertilised cell that then divides and grows into the baby animal or plant. So the offspring has half its chromosomes (and therefore half its genes) from each parent. It has, for example, a gene from its mother for eye-colour and a similar gene from its father. One of these two genes for eye colour may be stronger than the other and whichever it is will fix the eye-colour of the baby.

But remember that the mother also had two genes for eye-colour! And it is a matter of chance which of these two were passed on to the baby. The same is true for the father.

A diagram will help us here. Let us label the mother's two genes A and B, and the father's C and D. This is how they might be sorted out in the baby.

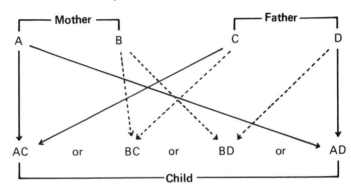

So we see that the baby's eye-colour genes may be any one of four different pairs. If four babies are born, each one could have a different pair of genes, and therefore different eye colour. The same is true of any other feature, like the shape of the nose or the thickness of the hair, and so on.

So a large amount of variation can happen because of the way the genes are assorted when egg and seed cells are made and when these cells join together to form a baby animal or plant.

If our diagram had gone back to the four grandparents of the baby (and if the number of possible genes for a particular feature is large enough) we would see how genes AB, CD, EF, GH in the four grandparents could give any one of 16 possible gene-pairs in the baby. After many generations, I think you can see, there might be hundreds of possible pairs of genes and each different gene-pair would produce a slightly different effect in the baby.

This is why no two babies are ever exactly the same. (Except identical twins who come from the same fertilised egg and so have exactly the same gene-pairs.)

It is obvious that this sorting out of genes can never make one kind of animal or plant change into another. However the different genes are sorted out, all the genes belong to that kind of creature. You do not get rabbit genes in hares or squirrels. You do not have monkey genes in man. All the genes in man are human genes and whatever differences may be found among people (light skin, dark skin, curly hair, straight hair, and so on) no human can be born with monkey's eyes or a gorilla's finger nails!

A limit to variation

The many variations that can happen in plants and animals can be very useful. Dog breeders, racehorse breeders and rose breeders all take advantage of variation.

Suppose a rose grower wants to breed a new variety of rose and wants it to be pink. He will take pollen from a white rose and use it to fertilise a red rose, knowing that some of the seeds that result may grow into pink roses. This is because the gene for red and the gene for white will pair up in some of the seeds and the two genes may balance to give a pink colour. (He will be unlucky, though, if either gene dominates the other. If red dominates white, all roses with one white gene and one red gene will be red. Those with two whites will be white and those with two reds will be red. None will be pink!)

By trial and error, then, the breeder crosses or breeds together animals or plants hoping to get offspring which have the best sides of both parents. Then they breed together the best of the offspring and so on, hoping to get a perfect plant or animal.

This is rather like natural selection, of course. Except that choosing by the breeder is much more sure than choice by nature. The breeder knows exactly what he wants and his choice of animals or plants to breed is not haphazard. So breeding should have the same result as natural selection except that it is much less chancy and much quicker. So natural selection should not be able to do anything that deliberate breeding cannot do.

What do breeders find? Of course, they are very good at breeding new varieties of flowers, grain, dogs, pigeons, racehorses and so on. But they always find a limit to what they can do. There comes a point where they can go no further.

A breeder of birds may be trying to produce birds with longer and longer tail feathers. A breeder of sheep may be trying to get thicker and thicker wool. Up to a point their efforts succeed. But there always comes a point where the long feathered birds either cannot lay fertile eggs or else their young hatch out with shorter feathers than their parents! In the same way the long-haired sheep become infertile or else their lambs revert (i.e. go back) to being short-haired. Breeding always has its limits.

If this is so, then natural selection must also be limited in what it can do to change animals or plants. Some changes can and do take place because of natural selection. But nature itself provides a fence around each kind that God created so that variation cannot pass beyond a certain point.

Swapping DNA

The second way that organisms can change or vary is by actually giving DNA molecules to one another. This has only been discovered very recently and only happens with bacteria (or germs). If two bacteria touch each other one of them can actually pass DNA to the other.

You may have seen on television a film where a supply ship comes alongside another ship and sends supplies of food and other things across by ropes slung between the two boats. This is a good picture of the way one bacterium passes DNA to another.

Some germs have DNA which helps them resist the medicines used by doctors to cure certain diseases. Sometimes these germs pass DNA to other bacteria, making them resistant to the medicines too. This is an example of change or variation caused by swapping DNA between organisms. Obviously, it cannot cause evolution in more advanced animals or plants.

Mutations

The third way that living things can vary is called "mutation". This is just the Latin word for change, but it is used in biology to describe a special kind of change.

From time to time, in any group of plants or animals, one is born quite different from the rest. An animal may be an albino, with pink eyes and white hair. It may have some deformity, like an extra leg. It may be ill because its body cannot make some necessary chemical. It may be a four-leafed clover.

These sudden changes are the result of mutations or accidental changes in the DNA codes.

Think again of the DNA codes as plans or blue-prints for the cells. It is as if someone has crept into the factory at night and altered one of the plans. Next day the factory (i.e. the cell), following the altered plan, makes those particular products wrongly. Or perhaps it cannot make them at all because the blue-print has been spoiled.

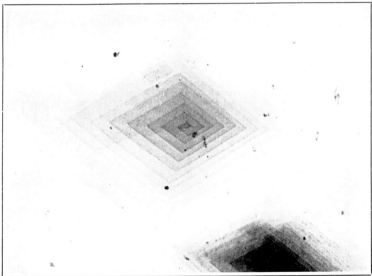

Plate 1. The beauty of the universe seen in the very large and the very small. A spiral nebula, thousands of light years across, and microscopic polymer crystals, each layer less than a millionth of an inch thick. (*Photo of nebula:* *Science Museum, London.*)

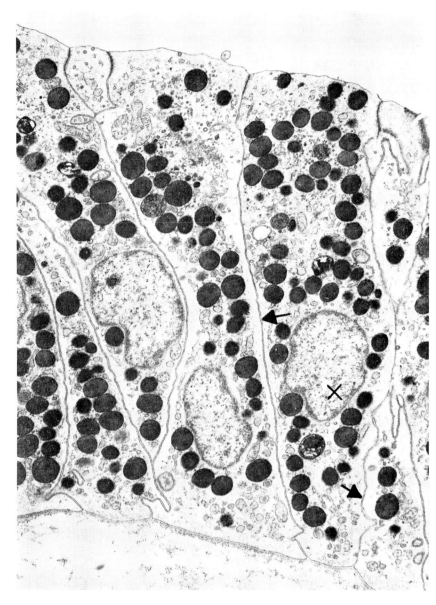

Plate 2. A group of single cells from a sea squirt. In one of the cells the nucleus is marked with a cross and the cell wall with arrows. Taken through the electron microscope and magnified about six thousand times. (*Courtesy of Dr. S. D. Prince.*)

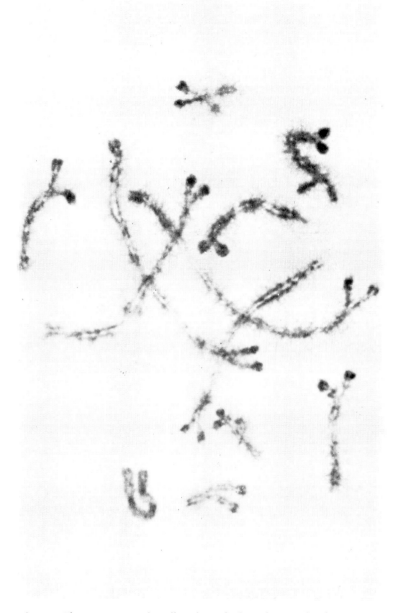

Plate 3. Chromosomes in the cell nucleus of a desert locust. The chromosomes are joined together in pairs and the fuzzy hairs sticking out from the chromosomes are strands of partly uncoiled DNA. (*Courtesy of Dr. J. Parker.*)

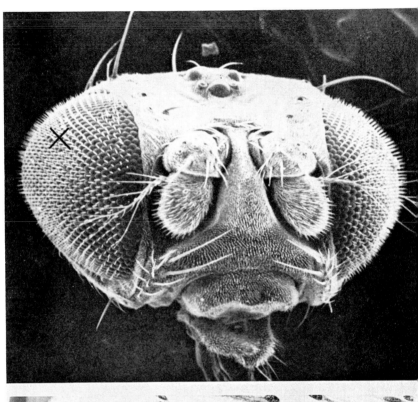

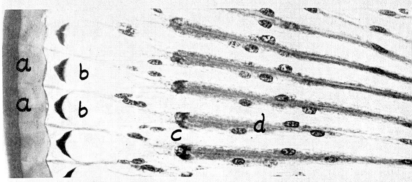

Plate 4. The complex eye of an insect. Top picture shows the head of a fruit fly with its huge compound eyes (one marked X). Bottom picture shows, at higher magnification, a cross-section through such an eye. Parts labelled (*a*) are the outer lenses (each small bump in the top picture is one lens); parts (*b*) are inner lenses; (*c*) are pigment cells and (*d*) are vision cells. (*Courtesy Dr. L. J. Goodman.*)

Plate 5. A whole fossil fish (*Lepidotus elevensis*), with its scales intact. (*Courtesy of the British Museum of Natural History.*)

Plate 6. A fossil tree-trunk at Cromford Canal open-cast coalmine. The tree is twenty-six feet high and passes through several coal strata. (*Courtesy of the Geological Museum.*)

Plate 7. Stalactites in a limestone cave. (*Courtesy of the Geological Museum.*)

Plate 8. Marine fossils (ammonites) in a limestone slab. (*Courtesy of the Institute of Geological Sciences.*)

Plate 9. Archaeopteryx fossil from Berlin. (*Courtesy of the British Museum of Natural History.*)

Plate 10. Skeleton of Tyrannosaurus Rex. (*Courtesy of the British Museum of Natural History.*)

Plate 11. Shod human footprints in Cambrian rock, Antelope Springs, Utah. A crushed trilobite, indicated by the arrow, can be seen in one of the footprints. According to evolutionary ideas man did not evolve until hundreds of millions of years after the Cambrian rocks were formed and trilobites became extinct. (*Courtesy of W. J. Meister, Jr.*)

Plate 12. Chalk cliffs formed from the skeletons of minute sea creatures. (*Courtesy of the Geological Museum.*)

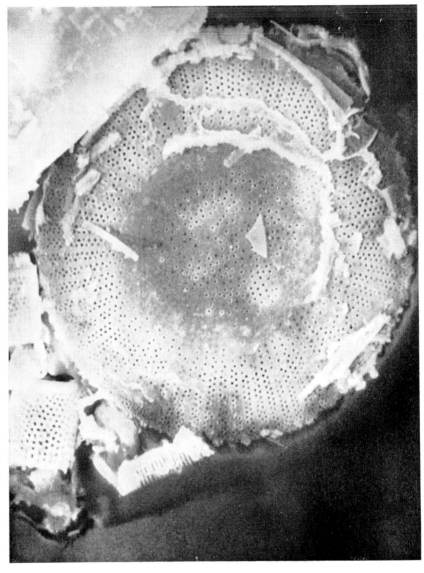

Plate 13.   One of the tiny sea creature skeletons from which chalk and similar deposits are formed. Magnified 5,000 times in the scanning electron microscope.

An albino animal, for example, is white with pink eyes, because it has lost the power to make colour or pigment molecules. The bit of DNA which usually serves as a plan for the pigment molecules has been altered in some way. The pigment cannot be made and the creature's eyes and hair have no colour.

Most mutations are harmful. That is, the organism which has the altered plans is less likely to stay alive or have offspring. This is nature's way of stopping harmful changes becoming wide-spread.

Some mutations do not cause any trouble because they only alter some unimportant feature of the plant or animal. A few mutations may be helpful. For example, a mutation which makes an animal white will give it an advantage in snow-covered country, because it will not be so easily seen by its enemies. In the same way black-coloured moths live longer than light-coloured moths of the same species in dirty industrial surroundings.

Although most mutations are harmful to the organism, evolutionists argue that about one in every hundred mutations is helpful. These few helpful mutations, they say, are kept going in the group of animals or plants by natural selection. In this way many small helpful mutations can add up and eventually cause evolution.

This seems a good argument. Since a mutation is a change in the blue-print, it is not like gene assortment which just shuffles the genes that already exist among the group. There is a good chance of real change.

But when we look more closely we find it is not so simple!

Mutations take too long

First of all it is a fact that organisms that have been studied in the laboratory (fruit flies and bacteria, for example) have never evolved into different kinds of creature. Thousands of generations have been bred. The mutations have been speeded up by using X-rays and chemicals. But although new varieties have been made, the fruit flies and bacteria were basically the same creatures as they were at the start.

Then again, it is found that mutations can be reversed. That is, the mutants can change back to the original forms.

But most important is the fact that even helpful mutations are not likely to survive in a group or population. It has been worked out that the chances of a gene mutation surviving are so small that it would take between a thousand and a million generations to replace completely the original gene.

That is just one gene. But a complicated creature like man has something like 20,000 genes, most of them different, as far as we know, from the genes of a chimpanzee!

From these and other figures it seems that for chimpanzees to turn into man would take at least twenty million generations, i.e. at least four hundred million years. And this is the shortest time it would take because it supposes that every helpful mutation is a step from chimpanzee to man! In fact almost all helpful mutations would be a step from chimpanzee to better chimpanzee. So forty thousand million years would probably be a better guess for evolution of man from monkey. But this is ten times the age that evolutionists give to the earth itself!

We cannot rely too much on this kind of arithmetic because so many of the figures used are just guesses. But evolutionary scientists freely admit that evolution by mutation and natural selection takes far too long to fit into the history of the earth. They still say it happened this way, however, and still hope to find some way to explain the time problem.

Neither mutation, nor natural selection, nor both together seem able to explain evolution. Evolutionists who are real scientists admit this in their scientific writings. Unfortunately those who try to explain evolution to non-scientists are not so honest. Or perhaps they have just not thought about it carefully enough.

Chapter 6

How old is the earth?

Evolution says that the earth must be very, very old because it would have taken thousands of millions of years for life to arise by accident. It would have needed more thousands of millions of years for the first life-form to evolve into the many different creatures and plants that now live upon earth.

So the age of the earth is very important to the theory of evolution.

There are two reasons why we must talk about the age of the earth in this book. Firstly, the scientists who study the earth (they are called geologists from the Greek word "geos" meaning earth), agree with evolution that the earth is very old. They believe it is about four thousand million years old, and say that this gives plenty of time for evolution to have happened.

Secondly, the Bible seems to suggest that the earth is not very old at all. If we go back through the names listed in the book of Genesis we can work out, roughly, that Adam was created no more than about ten thousand years ago. If we then accept that the seven days of creation in Genesis chapter one were ordinary days or short periods of time, we arrive at an age for the earth of about ten thousand years. It is not quite as simple as this, however, as we shall see later in this chapter.

So we need to look at the age of the earth to see if there *has* been enough time for evolution to happen and if there really is a contradiction between the science of geology and the Bible.

A timely tale

At first we may think that the earth must be extremely old because both evolution and geology say it is. Surely they cannot both be wrong?

In fact, they may both be wrong because geologists have used

C2

(and still do use) the idea of evolution to help them work out the age of the earth!

The story is told of a man whose job was to sound the hooter at a factory, telling all the other workers that it was time to go home. Every day at 1.00 p.m. for lunchtime and 5.30 p.m. for the end of work, he sounded the hooter. He did not use a watch or clock of his own because just across the street was a jeweller's shop with a large hanging clock outside. It could be clearly read from the workman's office.

At last the day came when the man retired from work. He decided he should go and thank the jeweller for his clock and the help it had been to him. When he told his story to the jeweller, who was himself an old man by now, a rather strange look came over the shopkeeper's face. After a pause he replied slowly . . . "But I always set that clock right by your hooter!"

I do not think the story is a true one, but it helps us to see the danger of evolution relying on geology for its time, and geology relying on evolution. Like the hooter and the clock, they could agree about the age of the earth and yet both be completely wrong!

Telling the age of the earth

I am sure you know how old you are. How do you know? The answer is, of course, that when you were born your parents were there to record the date and time of your birth. This date was also written down on your birth certificate. So it will always be possible for you to work out your age.

Working out the age of the earth is rather more difficult because there was no one there when the earth was "born". No one, that is, except God Himself.

How, then, can geologists work out the age of the earth? There are two chief ways that are used. Actually what is worked out is not the age of the earth itself but the age of the rocks that make up the earth's crust.

These rocks are of two main kinds. Firstly there are the "sedimentary" rocks which began as sediments, e.g. layers of mud at the bottom of the sea. These layers of sediment or mud were later compressed and cemented together until they turned into rocks like shale, limestone and many other kinds (see figure 12). It is only the sedimentary rocks which contain fossils.

Secondly there are rocks which became solid after being melted

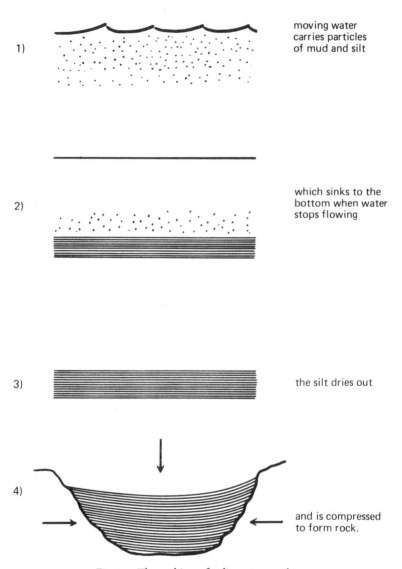

1) moving water carries particles of mud and silt

2) which sinks to the bottom when water stops flowing

3) the silt dries out

4) and is compressed to form rock.

Fig. 12 The making of sedimentary rock.

or nearly melted, in the hot interior of the earth. The best known example is lava which even today surges up from the depths of the earth when a volcano erupts. These kinds of rock are called "igneous", after the Greek word for fire.

A third kind of rock is called "metamorphic", which means it has changed its form. Metamorphic rocks may have begun as sedimentary rocks but have since been changed by heat and pressure. In this chapter we will group together the fire rocks and the changed rocks because neither of them normally contain fossils.

When we talk about the age of a rock, we really mean the time that has passed since the sediment was laid down (for sedimentary rocks) or the time since the rock last became solid.

How can these ages be worked out? The most up-to-date way is to study the radioactive elements in the rocks. We shall look at this more closely in a moment, but this method was only discovered about sixty years ago and before that geology relied on the rate of sedimentation to tell the age of the rocks.

This method is very simple. Suppose we measure what thickness of mud collects at the bottom of a lake in one year. We can do this by measuring the thickness of mud at the same place once each year. Suppose that one inch of mud is laid down in one year and that this would compress to half an inch if all the water were squeezed out.

We now find a mountain forty thousand feet thick, made of sedimentary rock. Suppose the sediments which built that mountain were laid down at the same rate as the mud in our lake. This would have taken forty thousand times twenty-four years to happen. That is, the lowest layers of rock must be at least ninety-six thousand years old.

To work out the age of the sedimentary rocks, geologists have to know two things. They have to know how much sediment has built up each year, on average, ever since the earth was formed. Then they have to know how thick are the sedimentary rocks.

How fast does sediment form? The answer is that it all depends when and where you measure it. Far out in the deep oceans, sediment forms very slowly, less than a foot in a hundred years. But we also know that a heavy flood can leave behind mud several feet thick in a few hours. We have a small river nearby which has to be cleared of mud every few years. Two or three feet of sediment collects in the river bottom in that time.

To work out the age of the rocks geologists usually use the very slowest rates of sediment build-up, like a foot in a hundred or a thousand years. They take it for granted that the sediments were formed very slowly in deep oceans and far from land. But if the sedimentary rocks were formed on or near land, by fast rivers or floods, they might have been made ten thousand times faster (see figure 13). That means their age would be ten thousand times smaller than the geologists say.

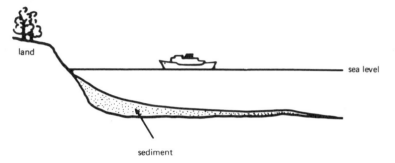

Fig. 13   Sediment builds up much faster near land than in the deep oceans.

Buried in the mud

Is there any way of telling whether the sediment or mud was laid down quickly or slowly? The answer is yes. The sedimentary rocks contain myriads of fossils or animal remains. These are not only fish and sea creatures but also mammals, birds, insects and other land creatures which would never be found far out in the deep oceans. These creatures were buried suddenly and often on land. There are far too many fossils for them to be just those creatures which happened to fall into rivers and lakes. Sometimes whole herds of grazing mammoths were buried so suddenly that grass was found in their mouths when their fossils were uncovered. It is obvious that the best preserved fossils were buried suddenly by flood waters, and the mud in which they were buried became the sedimentary rocks.

We cannot say that all fossils were buried in sediment laid down very quickly, but we can say that many, and perhaps most were. Even the hard parts of dead animals, like skeletons and sea shells, do not last long enough to be fossilized by very slowly-laid sediments. They are quickly broken up by the action of waves and pebbles unless protected by mud. Certainly whole fish, animals and birds would not be found as fossils at all unless they were buried very quickly indeed. Their bodies would have decayed or been eaten long before they could be buried if sediment collected at only one foot in a hundred or a thousand years (see plate 5).

There is another thing that shows that rock strata or layers must have been laid down in very short times. Sometimes fossil tree-trunks are found which pass through many different layers of rock (plate 6). Whether the different strata built up around the tree-trunk, or whether the tree was pushed down through several layers of soft mud after they were formed, does not really matter. In either case the layers of sediment must all have been about the same age. Otherwise the top end of the tree-trunk would have decayed long before it was buried, or else the lower layers of sediment would have been far too hard for the tree trunk to pierce them. These tree-trunks show us that up to thirty feet of sediment, containing four or five different rock strata, must have been laid down in a few years at most.

The fossils in the rocks, then, show us that at least some of the sediments were laid down quickly, probably by flood waters, rather than slowly as most geologists think. This means that a rock, thought to be a hundred million years old, might only be ten thousand years old after all.

Some strange arithmetic

I said that to work out the age of the rocks, we need to know how much sediment forms in a certain time and, secondly, how thick are the sedimentary rocks. We have talked about the first of these. Now let us look at the second.

The greatest thickness of sedimentary rocks, at any one place, is about fifty thousand feet. So we would expect the oldest sedimentary rocks to be no more than fifty thousand years old, if we take the fairly rapid rate of sedimentation of one foot each year. But geologists argue that really there should be ten times this thickness of rock, so that the age is ten times as great. This is how they work this out.

First of all, the rocks are divided into layers (or strata). Different layers are recognised by the different kinds of fossil they contain. The different strata are given complicated names but we can just label them A, B, C and so on. Layer A has a particular group of fossils and layer B a rather different group and so on.

The thickness of any layer is not the same in all parts of the world. In fact most of the layers are missing altogether in any one place. Layer K, for example, may be little more than a foot thick in England but twenty-four thousand feet thick in California, U.S.A.!

There is an obvious way to explain why layer K is so thick in California but so thin in England. It is that the sediment was laid down much faster in one place than in another. The one-foot layer would have built up very slowly and the twenty-four thousand foot layer very fast. But no, say the geological time-keepers. They say that the thickest part of layer K was laid down at the slowest rates measured today. The very thin K stratum, and the layers that are missing altogether, are supposed to have been worn away.

So, to get the age of the sedimentary rocks, they add together the greatest thicknesses of all the layers A, B, C and so on. They then say that all these thick layers were laid down at the same slow rate. In this way they work out that the true thickness of all the sedimentary rocks is nearly five hundred thousand feet, not the fifty thousand feet actually found anywhere on earth. Then they say these were all laid down at one foot in a thousand years, i.e. very, very slowly. So they arrive at an age of five hundred million years for the oldest sedimentary rocks.

But if we say instead that the thinnest layers were laid down at the slowest rate, and the thickest at a much faster rate, we would get ages in thousands instead of millions of years!

Why, then, do geologists say the rocks are hundreds of millions of years old, when they may only be thousands of years old? The answer is that they are trying to agree with the theory of evolution that needs enormous lengths of time to explain all the forms of life we know today. Evolution and geology are both setting their own clocks by the other's. They may both agree, but they may both be wrong!

Radioactive clocks

We must be fair to the geologists. They themselves agree that rock ages worked out from sediment build-up are not reliable. No one really knows how slowly or how quickly the sedimentary mud was laid down.

Quite recently, though, it has become possible to measure the ages of some rocks in a completely different way. Anything that measures the passing of time, can be called a clock. We all understand the kind of clock with hands and a dial, but there is also the hour-glass or egg-timer in which sand runs from one half of the glass into the other and takes a certain fixed time to do so. Yet another way of measuring time is to follow the position of the sun in the sky. But let us imagine a quite different kind of "clock".

Imagine there are a thousand people attending a ball in a large hall. You are watching them from a gallery. They all have wrist watches so that they know the time, but you have no way of telling the time. Suppose that the people in the ballroom have a secret arrangement that during each hour one out of every ten will leave. So at the end of the first hour, one hundred people have left and nine hundred remain. In the second hour one out of every ten again leave. That is, ninety go during the second hour and eight hundred and ten are left. At the end of the third hour another eighty-one have left and seven hundred and twenty-nine remain.

Figure 14 shows how the number of people left in the hall changes with the passing of the hours.

You can now use the number of people left in the ballroom as a kind of clock. By using the diagram you can find out from the number of people at any time, how much time has passed since the ball began. If you arrived some time after the start you could still tell how long it was since the beginning, just by counting the number of dancers still there.

But you could only do this if you knew two things. Firstly you must know how many people there were to start with. Secondly you must know the secret arrangement, i.e. that one in ten leave every hour. If only one in every five left each hour, the answer would be quite different.

Many of the earth's rocks contain radioactive atoms. These atoms can lose tiny particles and change into different atoms. The radioactive atoms are like the dancers in our ballroom, and the change of one atom into a different atom is like one person leaving the room (i.e. there is one less radioactive atom each time such a change takes place).

The rules by which radioactive atoms change (or decay) are exactly the same as the secret arrangement among the dancers. This means that the number of radioactive atoms goes down as time passes in just the same way as shown by our diagram. We could work out how long had passed since the ball began by counting the dancers left behind at any moment. In the same way we can tell how long ago the radioactive atoms started to decay, by counting the number left at any time.

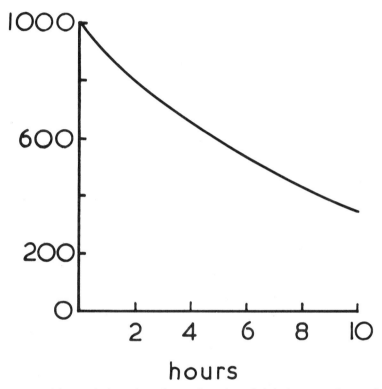

Fig. 14 This graph shows how the number of people left changes with time if a tenth of those remaining leave every hour. The decay of radioactive atoms happens rather like this.

Once again, of course, we must know two things: how many were there to start with and the secret arrangement by which they decay.

The second of these things is quite easy to find out by watching how quickly these particular atoms decay now. Of course we have to believe that the secret arrangement has not been changed since the beginning. We do not know for sure, but there is no reason to suppose that our atoms decayed at different rates in the past.

The secret arrangement of atom decay is most easily stated as the time needed for just half the atoms to suffer radioactive decay. In our ballroom picture the diagram shows that this time (or "half-life") is just six and a half hours. That is, after this time only about five hundred of the original thousand people would be left.

Different radioactive atoms have different half-lives. Some have half-lives of only a few seconds. But the radioactive atoms found in nature all have very long half-lives, up to many millions of years. Figure 15 gives a few examples.

ATOM	HALF LIFE IN YEARS
Potassium-40	1,260 million
Cobalt-60	5.28
Rubidium-87	50,000 million
Indium-115	600 million million
Platignum-190	1 million million
Lead-210	20
Lead-204	100,000 million million
Radium-226	1,622
Thorium-232	13,900 million
Uranium-234	252 thousand
Uranium-235	713 million

Note that atoms which are not radioactive have infinite half lives. So the half lives given above do not mean that the atoms have existed for millions of years. They could have been created yesterday and still have half lives measured in millions of years!

Fig. 15   The half lives of some radioactive atoms.

Dating the rocks by radioactivity

To tell the age of a rock (to date the rock) by the radioactive clock, we must first find a rock with a radioactive substance in it. Most rocks are not like this, so we have to look carefully. Secondly we have to be sure that none of our radioactive atoms have been lost since the rock was formed, except by radioactive decay. That is, none must have been washed out by water or lost as vapour from the rock. This makes things very difficult because most of the radioactive substances, like uranium and potassium-40, dissolve very easily in water. This is one reason why sedimentary rocks cannot be dated by the radioactive clock. Tiny particles of stone and clay are swept along by water before they drop to the bottom and form the sediment which later hardens into rock. While this is happening it would be easy for our radioactive substances to be washed out.

Even if this did not happen, the radioactive clock would not tell us how long ago the sedimentary rocks were laid down. The age we would measure would be the age of the tiny particles of rock and clay which make up the sediment in the first place. Needless to say, these particles are older than the sedimentary rock. There are a few special cases where the radioactive clock may give the age of a sedimentary rock, but usually it is impossible to date this kind of rock by radioactivity. Since fossils are only found in sedimentary rocks, it is clear that fossils cannot be dated by the radioactive clock.

To get around this problem, geologists measure the age of what are called "igneous intrusions". An igneous rock, remember, is one that has become solid after being melted. If molten rock is forced up from inside the earth it can push its way (or intrude) through many layers of sedimentary rock. The molten rock may even spread over the layers of sedimentary rock, forming a sheet of igneous rock, before it cools and becomes solid. Figure 16 shows how this can happen. Once again we can see this sort of thing today when volcanoes erupt and send streams of lava flowing across the countryside.

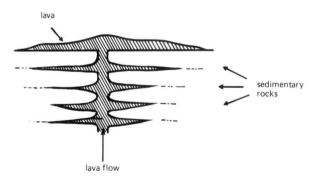

lava

sedimentary rocks

lava flow

Fig. 16   An igneous intrusion.

If we can find out the age of the igneous rock that has spread out over the sedimentary rocks, we know the sedimentary rocks underneath it must be older. So by measuring the age of an igneous rock by the radioactive clock we also get a least age for the sedimentary rocks beneath. If these rocks have fossils in them, we know the fossils must be older than the igneous rock.

Dating the fire rocks

How sure can we be of the ages measured on igneous or fire rocks by the radioactive clock?

These ages work out at thousands of millions of years. Can we rely on these ages? The honest answer is, no.

I must explain that the measurements themselves are done very carefully by very skilled people. The work has to be done very carefully using powerful scientific machines. This is because we have to detect a few radioactive atoms among millions of ordinary atoms. In spite of this I think we can rely on the actual measurements that are made. The trouble comes when we try to work out the age of the rock (i.e. the time since it was melted).

Think again of our ballroom. To work out the time since the ball began we had to know how many people were there at the beginning. In the same way, we need to know how many radioactive atoms were in our rock when it first became solid. But we have no certain way of knowing this! We have to guess or assume the answer to the question: "What exactly was in the rock to start with?" This guessing is done in several ways, depending on the particular kind of radioactive atom we are looking at.

One radioactive atom, potassium-40, decays or changes into another kind of atom called argon. If all the argon atoms in the rock today were once atoms of potassium-40, there is no problem. The number of potassium-40 atoms at the beginning would just be the number now added to the number of argon atoms now.

The trouble is, of course, that we have no way of knowing whether there were any atoms of argon there to start with. The rock-daters assume, or guess, that there was no argon in the molten rock. If there had been, of course, the real age of the rock would be much less than it seems.

The guess that there were no argon atoms to start with might be correct. But it might also be wrong. In fact molten rock could actually dissolve argon atoms from surrounding rocks or from the air.

There are several other ways of dating the fire rocks. One very clever method uses different rock samples from one area to work out what is called an "isochron". This is too complicated to explain in this book, but it is a method that seems to work without having to make any guesses.

When it is looked at closely, though, we find that guesses still have to be made. The guess, or assumption is different in this case. Instead of guessing how many radioactive atoms were in the rock to start with, we have to assume that different minerals in the same rock have the same proportion of radioactive atoms (for example, of an element called strontium). But this is just as much a guess as before. There is no radioactive dating method that does not need guesses or assumptions about what was in the rock at the beginning.

Another problem

There is another problem in dating the fire rocks.

A few years ago some lava from recent volcanoes was dated by the radioactive clock. Samples of lava were taken from different parts of the world. All were from volcanoes that had erupted during the past two hundred years. That is, all the samples were known to be less than two hundred years old.

The radioactive clock said that several of the samples were between a hundred million years and ten thousand million years old!

How could the clock be so wrong? We do not know for certain but it is likely that the guesses used in these cases were not very good. I should explain that an error of one per cent in our guessing can change the radioactive clock by hundreds of millions of years!

But there is another reason. Almost all rocks are mixtures of different minerals. When any mixture is melted some parts melt before others. If the heat is not strong enough some parts may stay solid and never melt. They just float around in the melted mass, like peas in a bowl of soup. This often happens with lava, so that the molten rock which flows from a volcano has lots of solid rocks in it. These rocks may never have melted since the earth began.

So when we try to tell the age of lava by the radioactive clock, we may not measure the time since the lava-flow at all. The lava may seem very much older than it really is because parts of it were not molten when the volcano erupted. Because of this it is possible that igneous rocks are much younger than their radioactive dates suggest.

If this is so, the sedimentary rocks found underneath the fire rocks will also be younger than they seem to be.

How old is the earth?

We have seen that none of the ways used to tell the ages of the rocks can really be trusted. The fossils would be explained more easily by a fast build-up of sediment than by a slow process. This means that the sedimentary rocks may be very much younger than people usually think.

The ages of igneous rocks, like lava, may also be much less than usually thought. This is because molten rock may always have some solid material in it. In any case, the guesses that have to be made in radioactive dating cannot always be trusted. A tiny mistake in these guesses can change the age of a rock by hundreds of millions of years.

Why, then, do all the measurements on rocks give the same sort of age? Why do all the rocks seem to be between ten million and four thousand million years old?

One possible answer is that evolution, together with the dates first worked out from sediment build-up, made everyone think that the rocks must be very old. When better ways were found to tell the age of rocks, like the radioactive clock, people already knew what sort of ages to expect.

Quite often the radioactive clock gives ages which are far too big or far too small. But because people know (or think they know) roughly what the age *should* be, these results are thrown away.

Stalactites and stalagmites

The usual way of working out the age of the earth is by trying to date the rocks. We have spent most of this chapter on that subject.

But there are other clocks or processes which seem to suggest that the earth is very, very old. The amount of salt in the sea, the thickness of chalk deposits, the wearing down of mountains by weather, these are all things that seem to say that the earth is millions of years old.

But this is only because people suppose that things happened in the past as slowly as they happen now. If the oceans had no salt in them to start with and if salt was always carried down to the sea by rivers as slowly as it is today, then it would have taken millions of years to make the sea as salty as it is. But these are big "ifs" and nobody really knows. The same argument is true for the other things I mentioned.

An interesting example is the growth of stalactites and stalagmites, the stone spikes that are found in caves (see plate 7). They are formed by dripping water which has calcium bicarbonate dissolved in it. As the water evaporates, the stone is left behind and builds up slowly into a spike.

Many of these spikes grow by only one cubic inch in a hundred years. If they had always grown as slowly, some must have taken a million years to reach their present size.

But recently it has been found that some stalactites and stalagmites are growing two hundred and fifty times as fast as this! At this rate the spike that seems to be a million years old would only be four thousand years old after all. Stalactites in coalmines and under road bridges in America have actually been measured growing as fast as one centimetre in twenty weeks. It is obviously silly to say that all stalactites and stalagmites grow very slowly. It is also silly to say that a big stalactite which is growing slowly now has been growing at the same speed for millions of years. Everything depends on the amount of dripping water, and this can change greatly from year to year.

To imagine that things always happened in the past at the same rate as they happen now is really very unscientific. It is certainly not a safe way to find out the age of the earth. Perhaps a story will help us see this more clearly.

Imagine that some visitors from outer space came to your town to find out what human beings were like. They can make themselves invisible, so they go about their work without anyone knowing. Because they have many different planets to visit they can only spend a week on their visit to earth. They are equipped with very good measuring machines.

Three of the visitors decide to work out how old human beings must be. They will do this by measuring the very small amount by which a person grows in just one week. Then if the person has always grown at the same rate, the age of the person (in weeks) will be found by dividing his height by the amount he grows in a week. Easy, isn't it?

So one of the visitors goes to a school and measures how much children grow in one week. Another goes to an office, where adults work. The third, by chance, finds himself in an old people's home. At the end of the week they all meet to compare notes.

The first one says that human beings are about four to five feet tall and grow at about four inches a year. They must therefore be about twelve to fifteen years old.

The second disagrees. He says human beings are five to six feet tall and grow so slowly that he could not measure the growth. He knows his machine *could* measure a growth of as little as a tenth of an inch a year. So he can say that human beings are at least six to seven hundred years old. They may be thousands of years old.

The third visitor has so far been silent. He looks at his friends and says, "You are both wrong. Human beings are getting smaller as time passes. My measurements show that their height goes down by an inch every five years. So it is impossible to tell their age from their height."

Of course, we know that only the first visitor, who went to the school, is anywhere near to being right. All the measurements were good, of course, but the idea that people grow at the same speed all through their lives is only correct for children. Even then the idea is not completely right, but it is roughly true.

But adults have stopped growing. Their speed of growth had slowed down before the visitors arrived to make their measurements. So the age worked out from their rate of growth now is far too large.

Finally, old people actually get shorter as they grow older. Again the rate of growth has changed and, in this case, has even reversed its direction. So their age cannot be worked out at all from their height.

I think this shows how dangerous it is to try to work out the age of the earth from the rate at which things happen today. This can only give the right answer if things always happened in the past at the speed they happen now.

But we know that many changes have taken place in the earth since its beginning. We know that mighty volcanoes, glaciers and rivers once flowed that have no counterpart today. We know the earth's climate has changed enormously during the past. We know that whole mountain ranges have risen and that continents have been swallowed up by the sea. How can we pretend, then, that things have always happened at the speed they happen now? The opposite is more likely to be true.

What does the Bible say?

I have tried to show that the age usually given for the earth (more than four thousand million years) is based on guesses of one kind or another. The guesses are usually made to give as much time as possible for evolution to have happened.

Because of this, there is no need to suppose that the book of Genesis is wrong when it suggests that the earth is very much younger than most people think. But what exactly does Genesis teach about the age of the earth? Christians disagree about this because Genesis does not actually tell us how old the earth is.

Some Christians try to make Genesis agree with geological time by saying that the six days of creation were not days at all but long periods of time. They would have to be about five hundred million years each.

Others say that the six days were ordinary days and that the earth is no more than ten thousand years old. We have seen that there is no scientific reason why this cannot be true.

A third possibility is that the six days were ordinary days, but that they began only when light appeared on earth. The earth was *there* a long time before the six days began but during this time, "The earth was without form and void; and darkness was on the face of the deep" (Genesis 1: 2).

How long the earth stayed like this we are not told. It could have been a very long time, allowing the surface to cool down enough for life to exist. This idea would also allow the igneous rocks to be very much older than ten thousand years. The creation of light on earth, the sky, the seas and life in all its forms would then have happened miraculously during the six days. The universe itself would have been created "in the beginning" and before the six days began.

I am not going to try to prove that one or other of these ideas is what the Bible really teaches. Each of the ideas gives us some problems. I do not accept the first idea (i.e. that the six days were millions of years long) because the only reason for accepting this is to make the Bible agree with evolution. Both the other ideas give full weight to God's work of creation, and so are ideas I can accept.

The second idea is, in some ways, the easiest. According to this, science can never be right about the way the universe and the earth were formed because this happened in a moment, by a single act of creation. The universe and the earth seem to be very old simply because God made them that way.

It is important to say that there is nothing in science to contradict this idea.

The third idea leaves God as creator of all things, but allows that the universe and the empty earth were created at some unknown time, "in the beginning". It allows time for the stars to be formed and for the earth to cool down from a molten mass. It allows the fire rocks to be much older than sedimentary rocks. This idea has a problem with verse 14 of Genesis one, which suggests that the sun, moon and stars were not created till the fourth day. Some people suggest that verse 14 describes the first appearance of these things in the sky, rather than their creation.

We shall have more to say about the six days of creation in the last chapter of this book. The important thing, of course, is that God created all things and that the Bible's story of creation is history and not a fairy tale. We may argue over what the Bible actually teaches about the age of the earth, but it will not matter as long as we understand that the Bible can be relied upon as being true.

Chapter 7

Fossils and prehistoric monsters

What are fossils?

Saltwick Bay is on the North Yorkshire coast close to the old fishing port of Whitby. Whenever I and my family are on holiday in that part of England we visit this spot because it is the best place I know for finding fossils.

A steep path leads down from the cliff top to the flat rocks which form the beach. Above these rocks tower the crumbling shale cliffs. Year after year, during the winter storms, new rock-falls from the cliffs throw tons of broken rock into the bay. In the freshly broken rock are hundreds and perhaps thousands of fossils.

Along the beach a little way, there is a huge fossil fish ten or twelve feet in length embedded in the rock and badly worn by storms and human feet! But it can still be recognised as a fish. An hour's search at Saltwick Bay (helped by a geological hammer for breaking open stones which may have fossils in them) is enough to find ammonites, belemnites, bivalves and fish in abundance (see plate 8).

What are fossils? They are remains of living things that were buried long ago in mud and silt. The mud or silt was deposited or laid down by moving water but was then hardened into rock by drying, heating and pressure.

Another way the silt can be turned into rock is by its grains being cemented together by other minerals as it dries out. If you live in an area where the water is hard you will know what I mean. As the water evaporates from your kettle it leaves behind a hard white material which is difficult to remove. The same material may also collect at the spout of a tap or in the bath under a dripping tap. The substance is calcium carbonate which comes from another substance, calcium bi-carbonate, dissolved in the water. When mud or silt dries out from water containing these or similar minerals, they act as a cement, sticking the particles of mud together into a rock-like mass.

Any creature which dies and is buried in mud may therefore finish up as a fossil in the rock. Of course the soft parts of the creature soon decay, even though protected by the mud. But as they decay, their place is taken by minerals from the water so that even the soft parts may be turned to stone and kept (or preserved) for us to see today. Often the tiniest details of animal skin or tentacles and the delicate markings on the leaves of plants and ferns can be clearly seen in fossils. In other fossils only a skeleton or hard shell has been preserved.

Another kind of fossil is formed when the tracks of an animal are preserved. This can happen if a creature makes footprints in soft mud which is then covered by more mud before it is all turned to rock. The line between the original mud (with the footprints in it) and the mud laid on top, may be a line of weakness in the rock. When the rock is broken open it splits along this line and reveals the footprints (see figure 17).

Most fossils are found in rocks formed from mud and silt. (These, remember, are the sedimentary rocks we talked about in chapter six.) Some interesting fossils, though, are preserved, not in rock, but in other materials. Many insects are caught in the sticky resin made by certain trees. The resin hardens around the insect and keeps the body from decay. Because the resin is transparent, the insect can be seen inside, perfectly preserved. These lumps of hardened resin are called amber.

Another material that stops the remains of animals decaying is peat. Anything which dies and falls into a peat bog may be preserved without decay for thousands of years. Finally, creatures buried in mud which then froze and stayed frozen, have been preserved for very long periods of time. The best examples of this are the woolly mammoths which have been found in Siberia. Whole herds of these animals have been found in the frozen earth, some so well preserved that grass and daisies have been found in their mouths thousands of years later!

Fossils and evolution

Fossils are like a history book of nature. The fossils in the rocks, the "fossil record", show us what plants and creatures lived on earth long ago. They also show where they lived. Fossils of animals

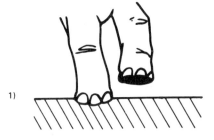

1)

Animal leaves
footprints in
soft mud.

2)

3)

Fresh layers of mud
are laid on top and
hardened into rock

4)

Later the upper
layers break away
or are washed away
to expose the footprints.

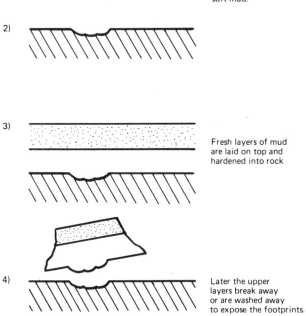

Fig. 17   How fossil footprints are made.

which now live only in hot countries have been found in cold
arctic lands. Most people agree that this shows the earth was once
warm all over.

So fossils can tell us a lot about the life and conditions on earth
long ago, when the sedimentary rocks were being formed. No one
disagrees about that. The theory of evolution goes further, however. It claims that the fossil record proves that evolution has
happened.

Fig. 18 Layers or strata of rock can often be seen in quarries and cliffs.

This has to be taken seriously, even by those of us who do not
accept the theory of evolution. The fossils, after all, are *there*! They
have to be explained. They are much more convincing than some
of the ideas put forward to explain how evolution might have
come about. In fact there are some people who believe that evolution did happen, because of the fossil record, but at the same time
do not accept that Darwin's theory explains how it happened.

So the fossils are the only real evidence for the idea that life has
evolved, changing from one form to another, over many millions
of years. Without the fossil record there would be no reason to
believe in evolution.

Let us see what the fossils really do tell us about life in the past.

The history book in the rocks
We saw in the last chapter that the sedimentary rocks were laid
down in layers. You can often see these layers in cliffs and stone

quarries today (figure 18). Sometimes the layers are tilted and folded because, after they were formed, the sedimentary rocks were squeezed, wrinkled and lifted by movements of the earth's surface. So some sedimentary rocks, once formed by flowing water, are now found at the tops of mountains!

Fossils of different kinds are not found mixed up in all the layers. Some layers have more of one kind of fossil than others. There is some mixing-up, but, by and large, the fossils are sorted out between the different layers. This means that a layer of sedimentary rock can be recognised by the fossils which are found in it.

Actually, this is the only way that the layers are now recognised because often there is no visible difference between the rock in different layers. The only difference is the kind of fossil found in the rock.

The different layers have been given names, and these names are shown in figure 19, together with some of the fossil creatures found in them. The oldest rocks would be expected to be in the bottom layers and the youngest at the top. The whole pile of layers makes up the "geological column" of rocks.

What, then, do the rocks reveal?

In the deepest rocks of all, the "pre-cambrian" layers, there are very few fossils at all. In the next layer up, the "cambrian" layer, are found the fossils of sea creatures like the trilobite and sponge. Although these seem to be some of the earliest of living things, they are really quite complicated and highly developed animals.

Working our way upwards through the layers we come next to other groups of sea fossils, like starfish, corals, snails and bivalves, followed by lung fish and sharks.

Higher up the geological column, in the so-called "carboniferous" layers, we find, for the first time, fossils of insects and amphibians (creatures which can live in and out of water).

Further up still, in the "mesozoic" (middle life) periods, are found fossils of reptiles, bony fish, toothed birds and dinosaurs.

Finally, in the upper layers of rock, which are together called "cenozoic" (recent life), we find the fossils of birds, mammals and man.

For plant life the picture is much less clear. It is almost impossible to build a geological column out of layers recognized by the fossil plants found in them. Some of the deepest layers contain plants very similar to those living today.

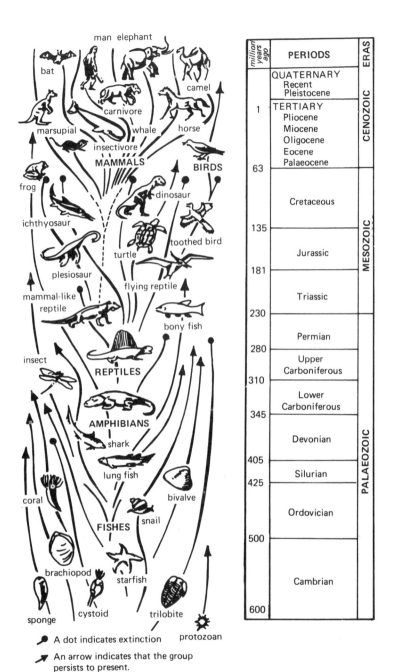

million years ago	PERIODS	ERAS
	QUATERNARY Recent Pleistocene	CENOZOIC
1	TERTIARY Pliocene Miocene Oligocene Eocene Palaeocene	CENOZOIC
63		
	Cretaceous	MESOZOIC
135		
	Jurassic	MESOZOIC
181		
	Triassic	MESOZOIC
230		
	Permian	PALAEOZOIC
280		
	Upper Carboniferous	PALAEOZOIC
310		
	Lower Carboniferous	PALAEOZOIC
345		
	Devonian	PALAEOZOIC
405		
	Silurian	PALAEOZOIC
425		
	Ordovician	PALAEOZOIC
500		
	Cambrian	PALAEOZOIC
600		

man elephant
bat
camel
carnivore
marsupial whale horse
insectivore
MAMMALS BIRDS
frog
dinosaur
ichthyosaur
toothed bird
turtle
plesiosaur
flying reptile
mammal-like reptile
bony fish
insect
REPTILES
AMPHIBIANS
shark
lung fish
bivalve
coral
snail
FISHES
brachiopod starfish
sponge cystoid trilobite
protozoan

A dot indicates extinction

An arrow indicates that the group persists to present.

Fig. 19 The geological column of fossil-bearing rocks, showing the names of the layers and their supposed ages.

Finally, we notice that many of the creatures found as fossils are extinct, that is, they are no longer found alive today. On the other hand some of the fossils from the deepest layers of rock, like the cambrian layer, are the same as creatures still alive now.

How evolution reads the rocks

Evolutionists say the fossils tell a story of slow change, from very simple sea creatures in the oldest rocks to very advanced animals in the youngest rocks. In pre-cambrian times, they say, life evolved from non-living molecules. At first these living organisms were soft and their fossils were not preserved. But gradually harder bodied animals evolved and the earliest of these are found as fossils in the cambrian rocks (which are said to be five to six hundred million years old).

As we go up through the layers, evolution claims, simple sea creatures changed (evolved) into fish, fish into amphibians, amphibians into reptiles and reptiles into birds and mammals. Mammals themselves then branched out into many different kinds including apes and, finally, man himself. But is this really what the rocks say? There are many reasons why this explanation of fossils is too easy. Let us look at them.

Firstly, there really is no slow change from simple organisms to complicated animals as we move up through the geological column. The "oldest" creatures found as fossils are as complicated as many animals today, and this is even more true of fossil plants and trees. In fact, some extinct prehistoric animals seem to have been larger, more powerful and more complicated than many modern ones. The fossil birds with teeth, for example, could not only fly, but also eat in the same way as advanced mammals like ourselves. Did today's birds evolve backwards from these beautiful creatures? (See plate 9.)

What the rocks actually tell us, of course, is that the fossils in the deepest rocks are *sea* creatures, i.e. those we would expect to find on the sea floor. Swimming sea creatures come next, followed by those equally at home in sea or on land (reptiles and amphibians). Finally land creatures and birds are found at the top of the geological column.

Secondly, it would seem that fossils are not being formed today. At least, not in the large numbers found in the fossil-bearing rocks.

It is not easy to describe the enormous amounts of fossil remains in the rocks. In some places there are so many fossils that these areas have been called fossil graveyards. A member of the United States Geological Survey, writing about one such area, says that "more than a billion fish, averaging six to eight inches in length, died on four square miles of bay bottom". In a single cave in Maryland, U.S.A. have been found fossils of dozens of different mammals including wolverine, grizzly bear, peccaries, tapirs, antelope, ground hogs, rabbits, coyotes, hares, beaver and muskrat.

Perhaps most striking of all are the graveyards in which complete shoals of fish or sharks, over large areas and sometimes numbering thousands of millions, have been buried suddenly, still in swimming positions. These fossils show that many of the remains we find in the rocks were not formed by the slow build-up of mud and silt that we see happening today. Rather, they were formed by great floods which suddenly engulfed whole shoals of sea creatures, or herds of animals, driving land creatures from their usual places to higher ground and bringing together animals from such different regions as arctic, tropical, woodland, grassland and river habitats.

If fossils are not being formed today in this fashion (and they are not), it may be completely wrong to imagine that the fossil record was formed slowly over billions of years. It is just as likely that most of the fossils were formed during a short and violent period of the earth's history.

Thirdly, the rock layers do not show a gradual change from one kind of creature into another. Fossils which are not found in deeper layers of rock appear quite suddenly in higher layers. There are no parent fossils linking the new fossils with more simple forms of the same animal.

A good example of this is the way that almost all mammal fossils suddenly appear in the "palaeocene" and "eocene" layers. In deeper layers, apart from a few pouched mammals, there are no remains. Then suddenly, in this double layer, appear a vast range of fossil mammals, including rabbits and hares, rodents, monkeys, bats, moles, dolphins, cats, dogs, pigs, camels, giraffes, deer, horses, elephants and sea-cows! Of course, it is still claimed that these layers of rock took thirty million years to lay down, but even if this is true, the rate of evolution must have been breathtaking.

What is more important, however, is that fossils linking one group of animals to another, and showing the pathway that evolution took, are completely missing.

Let us look more closely at this point.

The tree of evolution

We have all seen evolution pictured as a tree, as shown in figure 20a. The idea is that any animal or plant known today, or found as a fossil in the rocks, can trace its evolution back to the beginning through the twigs, branches and trunk of the tree. The tree of evolution is supposed to show how one stage of evolution gave rise to the next stage, and so on. Evolution is like a tree because a creature at one stage could evolve into two or more different creatures at the next stage. So evolution, like a tree, is always shooting out new branches. That, we are told, is why there are so many different kinds of living things today, even though life began as just a single tiny organism.

Like so many of the arguments of evolution, this sounds very convincing. Yet those evolutionists who are scientists have stopped using the tree to picture evolution. The reason for this is very interesting and I will try to explain it now.

Imagine an artist sitting down to paint a picture. The canvas in front of him is blank and empty. Soon it will be turned into a painting but at first it is just a blank sheet.

We can say two things about the blank canvas. Firstly, it has the ability to become a painting. Secondly, it has the ability to become any painting. We can call the blank canvas a general or generalized picture because it is not yet a special or particular picture. It is generalized because it can be turned into any picture the artist may choose to paint.

Once he has started painting, of course, things are different. Once he has started painting a landscape, he cannot change it into a portrait. Once he has started painting a ship at sea he cannot change it into a row of houses. So the canvas is no longer generalized. It has become special, or specialized, because the artist has chosen to paint one kind of picture on it rather than another.

Now all plants and creatures known to us are more or less specialized, that is, they have bodies with special rather than general features. Let us take an example.

Many creatures have four limbs. Humans have two legs and

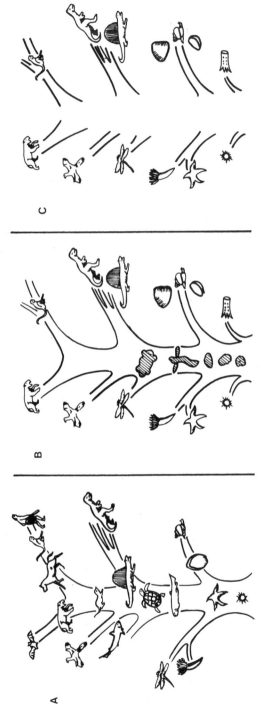

Fig. 20 The tree of evolution: (a) as it is often pictured; (b) as it should be, with only generalized creatures in the main trunk; (c) as it really is, without such creatures.

two arms, for walking upright and carrying things. Horses, sheep, dogs and deer have four legs specially for running and jumping. Birds have two wings and two legs, specially for flying and perching. Fish and dolphins have fins or flippers specially adapted for swimming. Each of these kinds of creature has limbs. But in each case these limbs work in different special ways.

Now try to imagine a creature with four limbs which are not specialized. It would perhaps have four stumps which so far have not developed anything special to do. Like the blank canvas, the stumps have the ability to become specialized. As the blank canvas can be turned into many different pictures, so the stumps can develop into different specialized limbs, for walking, carrying, swimming and so on.

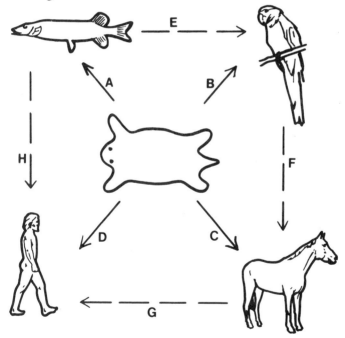

Fig. 21 Evolution can happen from generalized to specialized creatures (A, B. C and D) but not from one specialized form to another (E, F, G and H).

So we can imagine our generalized creature with its stumps evolving into a number of different specialized animals. This is shown in figure 21 by arrows A, B, C and D. These arrows show the generalized animal with stumps evolving into four different specialized creatures with different kinds of limbs.

What we cannot imagine is any of the specialized creatures evolving into another specialized kind. So evolution pathways shown by the broken lines E, F, G and H are not allowed. This is because the specialized limbs of, say, a fish would have to evolve backwards to the unspecialized starting point before setting off again towards a different kind of specialized form. There is no way that this could happen. The artist can, perhaps, wipe his canvas clean and start a different picture. But the theory of evolution itself forbids any wiping clean or backward movement from specialized to generalized forms.

What does this mean for the theory? It means that generalized creatures, like our stumpy friend in the diagram, are needed to explain evolution. Without such things evolution cannot happen, because one specialized animal is most unlikely to evolve into another specialized kind.

Now let us look again at our tree of evolution. Obviously the main trunk and branches of the tree must be made up of generalized creatures with generalized limbs, generalized skeletons, generalized organs and so on. Only such creatures could evolve into the many specialized forms of life.

So the specialized animals and plants must be the small branches and twigs on the outside of the tree. This is because *they* can only go on getting more specialized and cannot be the start of any big new step in evolution.

So our evolution tree looks like figure 20b, page 84, with generalized creatures in the centre and specialized creatures around the outside.

And this is where the trouble starts. You see, there are no generalized animals, either living or among the fossils. Even the oldest fossils are very specialized. So the middle of our tree is empty! We are left with the little branches and the twigs on the outside! There is no main trunk, there are no main branches! Our tree of evolution does not really exist at all. It should really be drawn (if we bother to draw it at all) as shown in figure 20c, page 84.

So the fossil record sets a very difficult problem for the theory of evolution. It is not what the fossils show but what they do not show that causes this problem. There are no fossils which even suggest that our generalized creatures ever existed. And if they never existed, evolution cannot have taken place.

Prehistoric monsters and the world-that-was

There is something specially exciting about prehistoric monsters. Perhaps you have seen their skeletons at the Natural History Museum or elsewhere (plate 10). Their enormous size and strength impresses us, of course. But I think we are even more fascinated by the picture they conjure up, of a world very different from our own.

We have already seen that the dinosaurs, ichthyosaurs and plesiosaurs (which together make up our prehistoric monster family), are just a few of the fossils that tell the story of prehistoric life on this planet. Very many other creatures, from sea creatures to birds and insects, have lived in the past but, like our monsters, have become extinct. The great number of extinct species, together with the vast coal beds formed from plants and vegetation, show that the earth was once much more fruitful than it is now. In fact we know that animal and plant species today are still dying out, but no new ones are evolving to take their place.

Fossils and experience show us, then, that life was once much more abundant on earth than it is now. They also show us that the barren arctic lands once supported great herds of grazing animals like the mammoths. Even tropical animals like lions, tigers, elephants and antelopes seem once to have lived over the whole surface of the earth. Coal and oil beds, formed from lush vegetation and, in the case of oil, the remains of sea creatures, suggest that plant life once ran riot on the earth. The vast thickness of chalk and limestone deposits also point to seas which teemed with tiny living diatoms.

Evolution claims that man was not there in this fertile, tropical world. He had not yet evolved. Yet fossil footprints in Texas, U.S.A. show human footprints alongside dinosaur tracks. Other human footprint fossils contain crushed trilobites, which are some of the oldest fossils known and supposed to have become extinct two hundred and thirty million years before man appeared on earth! (See plate 11.)

What changed the world-that-was into the earth as it is today? The evolutionist would claim that gradual changes of climate over millions of years were the cause. But that would make it impossible for man to have been present in that early luxuriant world. It would just have been too long ago.

The evidence of the rocks can be explained in another way. A terrible upheaval of the earth's surface may have taken place, causing enormous floods which engulfed the living world and changing the earth's climate completely. There is as much evidence to support this idea as there is for a very gradual change.

Only sudden, enormous floods can explain the existence of many fossils, as we have seen. In the normal way, no large number of birds or land animals could ever become fossilized. This is because they live, die and decay away from water. Only flooding can explain the vast numbers of such fossils found in the rocks. And only tremendous mud flows could possibly explain how millions of fish could be buried at sea in the very act of swimming.

We know also that volcanoes were very much more active once than they are now, covering thousands of square miles of the earth's crust with lava. Mountain ranges were formed by vast upheavals and folding of the rocks, while elsewhere the surface of the earth sank below sea level. Great masses of vegetation were swept together and exposed to great pressure to form coal beds. Much of the life on earth perished.

The Genesis flood

This is exactly the picture given to us by the Bible story of the flood in Genesis chapters 6 to 9. Some people believe that the flood was only a small one, and that the Bible has exaggerated what really only happened in one area.

But the events described in the Bible were not small, local happenings! Let us see this clearly from some verses of scripture.

"The Lord said, I will destroy man whom I have created from the face of the earth; both man, and beast, and the creeping thing and the fowls of the air; for it repenteth me that I have made them" (Genesis 6: 7).

"I will cause it to rain upon the earth forty days and forty nights; and every living substance that I have made will I destroy from off the face of the earth" (7: 4).

"The waters prevailed exceedingly . . . and all the high hills, that were under the whole heaven, were covered . . . and all flesh died . . . of fowl, and of cattle, and of beast, and of every creeping thing . . . and every man . . . and Noah only remained alive, and they that were with him in the ark" (7: 19–23).

In the New Testament, the apostle Peter adds, "By the word of God the heavens were of old, and the earth standing out of the water and in the water: whereby the world that then was, being overflowed with water, perished" (2 Peter 3: 5, 6).

We cannot, of course, be sure that all the sedimentary rocks were laid down by one, universal flood and that all the fossils were formed at that time. We can say, though, that only enormous, world-wide floods and upheavals, just like those described by the Bible, can really explain the changes that have taken place in the earth.

If most of the fossils were formed by the flood of Noah's time, how do we explain the order of the fossils in the rocks?

This is much easier than trying to explain them by evolution! The order of the fossils may simply be the order in which the creatures were trapped by the flood waters.

In the lowest layers of sediment we would find creatures of the sea bottom. Then next, swimming sea creatures, caught by the enormous amounts of sediment swept into the seas by water running off the land. Next in order would come river creatures and amphibians living near the water, then the slow-moving land creatures. Last of all to be overwhelmed by the flood would be the mammals, able to move to high ground and escape the flood until the last moment, and, of course, the birds. This is exactly what is found.

We would not expect the fossils to be in perfect order, of course, and in some places they would appear in different orders depending on the local situation. This is actually found in rocks where "older" fossils lie above "younger" fossils, a fact difficult to explain by means of evolution.

Finally, it is worth noticing that legends of a great flood are found all over the world and not just in the writings of the Jews (the Bible) and the Babylonians. There are similar but separate stories found in Persia, India, Burma, Indonesia, Tahiti, Hawaii, China, Japan, Siberia, Australia (among the aborigines), New Zealand (among the Maoris), Alaska, North America (among the Red Indians), South America, Egypt, Sudan, Nigeria, Zaire, South Africa, Greece, Iceland, Lithuania, Finland, Lapland, Wales and Ireland! This agrees with the Bible's claim, that from the three sons of Noah, "was the whole earth overspread (populated)" (Genesis 9: 19).

Chapter 8

Science, miracles and the Bible

A group of students was talking about science and belief in God.

"It is not possible for a scientist to believe in miracles," said the first, "because science shows there is no such thing as a miracle."

"That's right," said another. "Of course before science came along people had to believe in miracles because there was no other way to explain things. Now science can explain most things and in the end will explain even what we cannot understand today."

"I agree," said a third. "A miracle is only something we do not understand. Thunder and lightning are miracles to a primitive tribesman in the jungle. But we can explain them easily by science, so to us they are not miracles at all."

"Does that mean," asked another student, "that science makes it impossible to believe in God?"

"No," replied the first student. "It is possible for a scientist to believe in God, but not in a God who keeps interfering with the laws of nature to do so-called miracles."

"You are all wrong!"

The speaker was a fifth member of the group.

"You are wrong because you do not understand science. You are wrong because you do not understand miracles and you are wrong because you do not understand God."

The other students were very surprised. What they had said was, after all, what most people think.

"Explain what you mean," they asked.

The explanation took a long time. This chapter deals with some of the things that the Christian student might have said to his four friends. It is about the way we should understand science, miracles and God.

Things that science cannot do

The first book about science that I ever read was called "The

Marvels and Mysteries of Science". It is likely that I became a scientist because that book made such a deep impression on me when I was ten years old.

As the title of the book suggests, science is full of wonderful things. It has given us such a rich understanding of the world we live in, and such control over it, that we sometimes talk of the miracles of science!

Science has given us electricity and aeroplanes, medicines and machinery, transistor radios and television. Science *is* wonderful in the many things it has done.

But science cannot do everything and science cannot explain everything.

Some people are so enthusiastic about science that they think it will explain more than it can. They believe that everything can be given a scientific explanation and that no mysteries will stay unsolved for ever.

They find it very annoying when some things refuse to be explained by science. They are even more annoyed if you suggest that they can only be explained as the work of God.

Evolution satisfies these people because it seems to give a scientific explanation of the world, without the need for God. Those who think in this way do not really understand what science is. Here are some things about science that they forget.

How and why

Science can explain *how* things happen, but never *why* they happen.

If you ask me how a television set works, or how atoms link together to make molecules, I can answer your questions by science. In years to come it may be possible for science to explain many things that we do not yet understand, like the working of the human brain. But if you ask why electricity exists or why there are such things as radio waves, or why atoms behave as they do, science must answer, "That is no concern of mine". Science takes the world as it finds it and does not ask why things are what they are. That is a question for philosophy or religion.

Yet, really, the question "Why?" is more important than the question "How?". Of course we are interested in how things happen, but we can live perfectly useful and happy lives without knowing any science! After all, modern science, with all its

answers, is barely three hundered years old. Long before that
ancient civilizations rose and flourished without its help.

Man can live without science. But history shows that man
cannot bear to live without an answer to the question "Why?"
Why are we here? What is the meaning of life? Why do we love
some things and hate others? Why do we feel such things as fear
and guilt, love and happiness? What is the source of man's quest
for knowledge? Why do we explore our world and our universe
as we do?

These questions, and many others like them, are more important
than the questions that science *can* answer. It is obvious, then, that
the help we get from science is limited to certain parts of life.

Right and wrong

Science cannot choose between right and wrong. Science unravels
the mystery of physical life, but it tells us nothing about spiritual
life. It can unlock the power of the atom, but it cannot help us
choose between good and evil ways of using that power.

Words like "good", "evil", "right" and "wrong" do not belong
to the language of science at all, at least, not when they are used
to describe human desires and actions. How can science tell us it is
wrong to steal or right to help other people?

Many thinkers have tried to find a foundation in science for the
ideas of good and evil. They have tried to find in science a guide
to right behaviour. These people call themselves "scientific
humanists" because they think science can teach humans how they
ought to live. But they have not found an answer to their search.
Science has nothing to say about good and evil, beauty and ugli-
ness, truth and error, justice and mercy.

There is a very simple reason for this. Science is the study of the
physical world, but things like love, truth, justice and goodness
belong to the world of the spirit. They do not belong to the
physical or material world at all. So science does not concern itself
with them.

You would not go to a dentist if you had a pain in your leg.
You would not ask a doctor how to mend a motor car (see figure
22). If you did, they would say, "You have come to the wrong
person. If you want help and advice you must go to someone who
has the kind of skill needed to solve your problem."

So it is with science. We should not ask science to tell us what is good or evil. We should not expect science to guide us in our lives. Science is the wrong place to look for help in these matters. For these things we have to look elsewhere.

Fig. 22 You would not ask a doctor how to mend a car.

Though science cannot help us in these matters, the Bible can. The psalmist David says, "Thy word is a lamp unto my feet, and a light unto my path" (Psalm 119: 105).

Beginnings

Science cannot explain beginnings.

Beginnings (or origins) cannot be explained by science because they mark a change from what was to what is. Science studies the world as it is today, but it cannot work out what existed before the world or universe began.

Suppose no one had ever seen a caterpillar, but only butterflies and moths. No amount of study of the butterfly would ever show that this lovely winged creature came from a crawling caterpillar.

To some extent, of course, scientific study can tell us what has happened in the past. This is because the past leaves its mark upon the present. So we can count the growth rings in tree trunks and find that some trees are over three thousand years old. But we can only do this because trees have been growing in the same way for the past three thousand years. That is, today's world is the same kind of world as yesterday's, and this is true for many thousands of years of past history.

But the beginning of the world is a quite different matter. Science cannot tell us how the universe came into being. What was there before the universe? If the answer is nothing, where did everything come from? Or if there was something there before the universe began, what was it?

Science cannot answer these questions because it can only study what is happening now. It can only reveal the past if what happened then is like what happens now. That is clearly not the case with beginnings.

To get round this problem some scientists suggested that creation *is* happening now. They had the idea that atoms are being created out of nothing all the time in outer space. These new atoms would be so few and far between that we could never detect them. But it would mean that the universe never had a beginning, so there would be no need to explain one.

Scientists themselves do not now believe this theory of "continuous creation". There are many scientific reasons for thinking that the universe did have a beginning. What was there before the beginning, science cannot tell us and never will.

The laws of science

Finally, science cannot even explain itself! Let me tell you what I mean by this.

Science works by putting up theories to explain the facts that are seen or observed. Then each theory is tested by making more observations, or experiments, until the scientist is sure that his theory is correct. A theory that is very well tested is called a law of science.

We have the law of gravity, the laws of chemistry, the laws of optics and so on. Sometimes a law of science is known by the name of the scientist who discovered it (e.g. Newton's laws of motion).

It is the work of science, then, to describe the world around us by laws. Some of the most important laws, for example, say that matter and energy cannot be completely lost or gained, whatever happens. Other laws tell us how heat and work are related to each other, or how atoms join together to form molecules and crystals.

Now when I say that science cannot explain itself, I mean that it cannot explain where these laws of science came from. It cannot tell us why they are what they are and not different in some way. Let us take an example.

One well-known law tells us how the volume of a sample of gas changes if the pressure on it is changed. This is called Boyle's law and it says that the volume multiplied by the pressure is always the same, as long as the gas is not heated or cooled. This is written:

$$P \times V = \text{constant} \qquad \text{(a)}$$

So if pressure increases, volume decreases so that pressure times volume is the same as it was before (see figure 23).

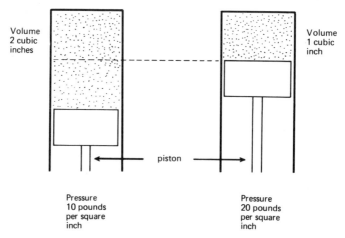

Volume
2 cubic
inches

Volume
1 cubic
inch

piston

Pressure
10 pounds
per square
inch

Pressure
20 pounds
per square
inch

Fig. 23   Boyle's law of gases; pressure times volume is constant if the temperature does not change.

You can imagine different laws that might have been true. For instance, pressure times the volume squared, might have been always the same.

$$P \times V \times V = \text{constant} \qquad \text{(b)}$$

Why is law (a) true and law (b) not true? Science cannot answer that kind of question. It tells us that (a) is true and (b) is false, but it can never tell us why.

For every law of science then, there are a very large number of possible laws that are not true. If there are a million pebbles on a beach and you choose just one of them, it means you are refusing or rejecting all the others.

Who chose certain laws instead of all the other possible laws? Why is nature like it is, and not otherwise? Where did the laws of science come from?

In a moment we will be answering that question from a Christian point of view. But everyone, whether Christian or not, has to agree that science cannot answer it. Science cannot explain itself.

So we have seen that science is limited. It cannot explain everything and never will be able to. As I write these words I have a wonderful view, through a large window, over Lake Windermere in Cumbria. It is a big lake containing a huge amount of water. I can see yachts and other boats sailing freely over the waters, exploring the inlets and islands or else running before the wind on the open reaches of the lake.

Science is like that. It holds a vast amount of knowledge. Like a very deep lake, it may even be too deep to fathom, to measure, with our little minds. Science has a great number of exciting corners to explore, but also has the wide open spaces, the galaxies and stars, as its playground.

But, like the lake, science also has its shores, its boundaries. The lake is limited in size by the mountains which surround it. So science is limited. There are shores which it cannot pass and mountains which it cannot enter. In these last few pages we have been tracing out some of these boundaries which science cannot cross. Only those who do not understand science will pretend that it can lead us into *all* knowledge and *all* truth. It obviously cannot.

Understanding God

What is God like? Nearly the whole Bible is taken up with this question and we are not going to answer it fully here. But there is one thing about God that we need to know if we are to understand miracles and how they can happen. This one thing is said most simply in the words of the Bible itself: "Upholding all things by the word of his power" (Hebrews 1: 3); "By him all things consist (hold together)" (Colossians 1: 17).

Both of these verses refer to Jesus Christ, the second Person of the Holy Trinity. But it is enough for us that they describe the way God relates to the created universe.

Many people, who do believe that God created the universe, are muddled about this. They think that He made the worlds at the beginning and then left them to run on their own. God is pictured as a great watchmaker, who made the creation like a beautiful piece of machinery, wound it up and left it to itself.

The trouble with this idea is that it leaves God out of His universe. He was there at the beginning, they say, but He isn't needed any more. The universe runs on its own, by the laws of science, the rules that He laid down in the beginning. Of course, this does explain where the laws of science came from. But it makes anything that God does *now*, an interference with the world. It is as if the watchmaker kept changing his mind after he had finished the watch and kept opening it up to alter its works! God becomes either a very distant Being, with no interest in the world today, or else He is a meddler!

This is not the teaching of the Bible. Let us see what the two verses quoted earlier tell us.

God is here

The first thing we notice is that both verses are in the present tense. They do not say that God used to uphold all things, or that all things started by being held together by Him. They say that He upholds everything now, even at this very moment.

This means that in a very important way, God is here. He is here now. If He were not here now, all things would not be held together and everything would not be upheld. This can only mean one thing. It means that the whole created universe depends on the presence of God for its existence. As Paul said, "In him we live and move and have our being" (Acts 17: 28).

If God stopped upholding all things, the universe would stop existing. It would simply vanish. This is a startling idea, I know. We feel that the world around us is so solid and so lasting. We also feel that God is vague and elusive. But really it is the other way around. The world exists because God exists and because, moment by moment, He holds everything together.

Seen in this way, the universe is less like a watch made by the watchmaker and more like the expression on the watchmaker's face! A watch is something separate from its maker. If he dies, the watch is not affected, it goes on just the same. But the look on the watchmaker's face is part of the watchmaker himself. He can change it whenever he likes. It cannot exist without him!

Can this solid, lasting world really be so flimsy as I have suggested? Isn't this view of the universe difficult to believe? Perhaps it is difficult for the non-scientist. But it should be easy for a scientist because he knows that the "solid" world around us is not really solid at all! Only a tiny fraction of the space occupied by an atom is really filled. The rest is empty. If all the matter in Mount Everest were compressed into the actual space needed by the protons, neutrons and electrons of which the mountain is made, how big would Everest be? The answer is, about the size of the armchair in which I am sitting (see figure 24). So our solid world is not so solid after all!

Fig. 24   Mount Everest would shrink to the size of an armchair if all the space inside its atoms were squeezed out. Something like this actually happens in a neutron star.

Another thing is, of course, that God is such a great and wonderful being that the world really is quite safe. It is not going to disappear accidentally because He goes to sleep or forgets to uphold it for a moment! The idea that the universe is like the expression on the watchmaker's face is not, therefore, a very good picture. But then it is difficult to think of any picture to illustrate the wonderful relation between God and His creation.

A mistake to avoid

In saying that the world and nature do not exist apart from God we must not think that nature *is* God. People who say that God is nature, and nature is God, are called "pantheists". They are wrong because they make God smaller than He is. According to them, God is not a person, but only a mysterious life-force working in nature. This idea cannot explain the beginning of the universe because, if God *is* nature, He could not have created it. He could not have been there before the universe existed.

The Bible teaches that God is above nature. He upholds nature, and the natural world could not exist without Him. But He existed before the universe began, and will exist after it has gone. He does exist apart from, and above, nature. Nature depends on Him, but He does not depend on nature.

The laws of science

Our two Bible verses not only say that God upholds all things but that He does it by "the word of His power". What is "the word of His power"? Christians often call the Bible the "word of God" and at the beginning of John's Gospel Jesus Christ is also called "the Word". But it is clear that neither of these meanings is intended here.

We have seen that the laws of science describe how things hold together in nature. They describe how atoms hold together and how things we can measure relate to one another. So, from the viewpoint of science, we could say that the laws of science uphold all things, or that all things hold together by these laws. (It would be more true to say that the laws describe how these things happen.)

These thoughts can all be brought together by one simple idea, which is this: the laws of science *are* the word of God's power!

You may have played a party game where one person is blindfolded and has to find or do something that he cannot see. He is given instructions by one of his team, who is allowed to say "forward", "backward", "left" or "right". So by talking all the time, and giving instructions, the guide leads the blindfolded person to find the object or perform the task, whatever it might be. At the same time, the blindfolded person obeys the words of his friend.

This is a very faint picture of the way God guides the natural universe by the word of His power. Moment by moment He tells the atoms, the molecules, the forces, and all the changing quantities of nature, what to do. They, in their turn, obey His voice.

Of course, God does not speak actual words to them. It would be nearer to say that He directs them by His thoughts rather than by words. But whatever picture we use, the whole universe not only exists because God wills it to exist, but it behaves the way it does for the same reason.

We could imagine, I suppose, that God might keep changing the way He did things. If this happened, there could be no science, because the laws of science would keep changing from day to day. But the Bible teaches that God is the author of order, not confusion. He wills, or orders, nature to work in a consistent or regular way. Because of this we can talk sensibly about laws or rules for the working of nature, and science can go about the task of finding out what these laws are. Because God is dependable, the laws of nature are dependable too.

So from the Bible we are able to answer two of the questions that science could not. How did the universe come into being? It was created, out of nothing, by the power of God. We should notice also that time itself is part of that creation. God is not subject to time. He is time-less, without beginning or ending. As an astronaut looks down on the earth, with its great distances from one place to another, so God looks down on the whole of time, seeing it all at once. "One day with the Lord is as a thousand years, and a thousand years as one day" (2 Peter 3: 8).

The second question science could not answer is: "Where do laws of science come from?" We now see that these laws are the moment-by-moment will of God. The atoms dance at His command and, even in their normal course, the winds and waves obey Him.

Miracles

The word "miracle" can be used in different ways. We may describe a miracle as anything science cannot explain. In that case we have already seen that the world is full of miracles. The beginning of the universe was a miracle, even by this meaning of the word. The laws of science are also miraculous, because they cannot be explained by science itself.

But when we use the word miracle we usually mean more than this. It is true that a miracle cannot be explained by science. But we also mean that whatever happened took place because God willed it for some special reason. Jesus turned water into wine to show His power to His disciples. He raised Lazarus from the dead to show His control over life and death. More important than all other miracles, Christ Himself came to life after His crucifixion to show that His sacrifice had been accepted by God the Father. Also, of course, being God as well as Man, Jesus could not possibly stay dead. If He had, it would have shown that all His claims were false.

The Christian faith cannot stand without miracles. If miracles cannot happen, then Jesus did not die and rise again. And if Christ did not rise from the dead, the Christian faith is empty of all meaning. As Paul says, "If Christ be not risen, then is our preaching vain (empty), and your faith is also vain" (1 Corinthians 15: 14).

Strangely, some Christians accept the theory of evolution to avoid saying that creation was a miracle. They seem to think that Christianity without miracles will be more easily accepted by the world. But there is no Christianity without that great miracle, the resurrection of Jesus Christ. At least, the Christianity of the Bible cannot exist without it.

Of course there are quite a lot of other miracles recorded in the Bible besides the ones I have mentioned. Some of those miracles are, perhaps, more difficult to believe than others. Some are more easily "explained" than others. But the important thing to see is that miracles can happen and did happen. Otherwise the Christian faith is hopelessly wrong and without foundation.

The atheist, who does not believe in God at all, would say that miracles do not happen and that the Christian faith *is* false. At least, such a person does not contradict himself. The so-called Christian who does not believe in miracles does contradict himself. You cannot have Christianity without miracles.

Understanding miracles

So miracles are vital for the Christian faith. But how can we accept miracles *and* the picture of nature that science gives us? Don't miracles contradict science? Is it really good enough to imagine

God meddling and interfering with nature to perform a miracle now and again?

As long as we think of God being somehow outside of nature, miracles will always seem wrong or unfair. But we have already explained that God is not outside at all! The laws of science are His thoughts, His commands. And they are His commands to nature moment by moment. God is here upholding all things and holding all nature together in the harmony of what we call scientific law.

So a miracle can take place at any moment. God has only to give different orders or commands to nature for as long as it takes the miracle to happen.

Seen in this way a miracle is no different from the normal course of nature. Both are the moment-by-moment will of God. Both are the word of God's power at work. They seem different only because God *usually* orders nature to work in a certain way, the way described by our scientific laws. From time to time, however, He commands nature to work in a different way. He does this for His own purposes and we say a miracle has taken place.

I travel from my home in Hertfordshire to London every day, except Saturdays and Sundays. I travel by train, because that is most convenient for me. Anyone who watched my travellings month after month could easily work out rules or laws to describe my movements. The law would say, "He travels by train for five days, one after the other, and then does not travel for two days. Then the same cycle is repeated." About once or twice a year, though, I travel to my office at London University by car. I usually have some special reason for doing so.

Our watcher (or observer) would be puzzled. He would see that the law, which describes my travelling habits, had been broken at those rare times when I travel by car. This is a picture of the way a miracle breaks the laws of science.

But my journey by car is really no different from my journeys by train. It *seems* different because I have, for just one day, broken my usual habit. Both the journey by car and the journeys by train are, however, my deliberate choice. That choice is made, day by day, to suit my own convenience and will. In this sense, both the usual train journey and the unusual car journey are the same.

So God usually orders nature to work in the way we understand by science. But sometimes, for His own good purpose, He changes

His orders. When He does this, our scientific laws do not apply. They are contradicted, and we say a miracle has taken place. That miracle, though, is no more strange than my choosing to travel by car one day, instead of by train!

Scientific laws and miracles are, equally, the will of God at work in nature, for He upholds all things by the word of His power. Seen in this way miracles neither contradict science nor go against our common sense. Miracle and scientific law are just two sides of God's constant working in nature.

In the next, and final, chapter of this book we are going to see how miraculous beginnings blend with scientific processes to tell the wonderful story of creation. I hope this chapter has helped us to see that we can mix miracles and science together without making nonsense. In fact, it is only when we *do* mix miracles and science in this way that we can make any sense of the beginning of the world.

Chapter 9

The miracle of creation

In this final chapter we will see how miracle and scientific law both have their place in the story of creation. As we saw in the last chapter, this working together of miracle and science seems natural and logical once we have understood what scientific law really is.

There is still a lot that we do not know about the way God created the worlds. There are many things that science cannot tell us and many things the Bible does not tell us. We must realise, then, that we will never know just how God did certain things at the beginning. We must also understand that people will disagree about the way things happened during the creation. They will disagree about the way we should understand or interpret the first chapters of the book of Genesis.

In spite of this, it is still possible to tell the creation story in a way that agrees with both true science and the Bible.

Genesis and history

Many people try to force science and the Bible to agree about creation by saying that the book of Genesis is just a myth, a piece of folklore. They say that this myth teaches a truth, but is not true history. It is a parable, they say, teaching *that* God created the universe but not *how* He did so.

Now this comes very close to saying that the Bible is not true. For Genesis does tell us quite a lot about how God created the world! There are, of course, some parts of the Bible which are parables. There are some parts which are poetry and are not meant to be taken as literal. But Genesis is not that kind of book. Genesis is a history book and the writer obviously believed that what he wrote had really happened.

To say that Genesis is just a parable is not the right way to make science and the Bible agree. The right way is to understand what

science really is and what the Bible really is. The Bible is what God
has chosen to reveal to man. It is true, and can be trusted in all
matters. Science is the study of the way God "upholds all things
by the word of His power". Because of this, science leaves room
for miracles to happen. Our last chapter has already shown us how.

Our description of creation will follow the first chapter of the
book of Genesis. It is only in this chapter, and other Bible refer-
ences, that we can see both miracles and science at work. If you do
not already know the first two chapters of Genesis well, it would
be useful to read them again now.

In the beginning

These are the first words of the book of Genesis, and they speak
of the beginning of the creation. They do not mean the beginning
of God, for the Bible teaches that God has neither beginning nor
ending. He is eternal.

When we use a word like "beginning" we are using the idea of
time. If time did not exist, words like "beginning" and "ending",
"before" and "after" would have no meaning. That is why God
can have no beginning. He created time along with space and all
that fills it.

Science tells us that our world exists in time and space and that
time and space are joined together in some very interesting ways.
They are not completely separate as we often think. They are both
part of a single "timespace" in which our universe exists.

When you switch on a television set, the picture exists only on
the flat screen. If you draw a picture, it also exists only in two
dimensions on paper. Anything solid exists in three dimensions of
space. It has height and length and breadth. It also has an age. This
means that it has a fourth dimension, the dimension of time. So
the universe itself exists in the four dimensions of timespace (three
dimensions of space and one of time; see figure 25).

God is outside of time, just as He is outside of space. God was
there before time began. There was no universe, no space, no
time, but only God. He lived then, as He lives now, in what the
Bible calls eternity. This is a realm beyond timespace, a realm we
find it very hard to imagine or think about. The Bible calls it
heaven. Unlike our material world it has neither time nor space.
Although God was alone in that spiritual world, He was not

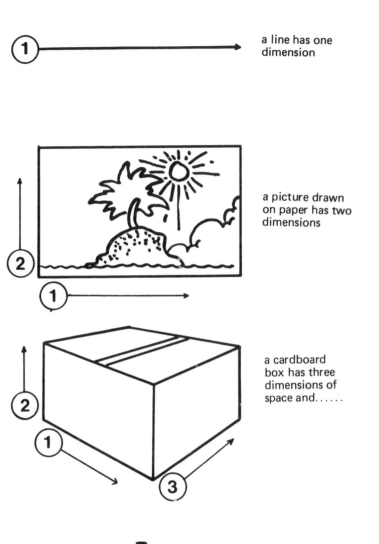

a line has one
dimension

a picture drawn
on paper has two
dimensions

a cardboard
box has three
dimensions of
space and......

like everything else ....

one extra dimension, age or time

Fig. 25 The physical world exists in space-time.

lonely. He always existed as three persons, Father, Son and Holy
Spirit and He had perfect fellowship with Himself.

But, for His own reasons, God did not wish to stay alone. First
He made the angels and other spiritual beings. They all lived (and
still live) in the spiritual realm. This includes those angels that
became proud and rebelled against God. They were put out from
God's presence and became devils. These are some of the things
the Bible tells us, but there is obviously a lot more that we are not
told about the spiritual world.

Then, for His own good reasons, God decided to make the
material universe. At that moment, time and space, matter and
energy, together with the laws they obey, came to exist.

We have seen before that science can tell us nothing of that
beginning-to-exist. Science can only explain what obeys scientific
law. It cannot therefore explain how those laws began. We must
either say that God made them begin, or else we must give up
trying to explain them at all.

But as soon as space, matter, time and energy *had* been created,
they would obviously all begin to obey scientific laws. This is just
because these laws were part of the creation. It is not possible to
imagine matter being created without the laws which control the
atoms, neutrons, electrons, etc., which make up that matter.

So it is quite proper for science to ask the question: "What was
the universe like when it was first created?"

The favourite theory today is that the universe began as a
gigantic fireball and that the galaxies and stars are just the remains
of that enormous explosion. Of course, we have to test this "Big
Bang" theory of how the universe began by seeing if it agrees
with what God has revealed in the Bible. But the point I want to
make is that once matter had been created it is quite all right to
start using scientific laws to describe what happened next, even
though there were more miracles still to come.

The universe

What does the Bible tell us about the creation of the whole universe? Is the "Big Bang" theory correct? If not, what *does* the
Bible say?

The Bible does not use the word "universe". It speaks instead
of "the heavens" or "heaven". The Hebrew word means "the

lifted-up things". This word is used in three different ways in the Old Testament.

Sometimes it just means "sky". In Genesis 1 verse 20, for example, the birds are said to fly in the heavens. Sometimes it means the spiritual world where God lives. But sometimes it means the things we can see in the sky but which are far, far away beyond the sky, things like the sun, the moon and the stars. When the words "heaven" or "the heavens" are used in this way, they describe the whole universe. Here is an example from Psalm 8: "I consider thy heavens, the work of thy fingers, the moon and the stars which thou hast ordained . . ." (Psalm 8: 3).

Whenever the Bible speaks of "the heavens and the earth" it probably means the universe and the earth. The heavens are put first because the universe is much bigger than the earth and also, perhaps, because the universe came first in the order of creation.

The idea that the universe came first agrees with scientific ideas of the history of the universe. But it seems to disagree with verses 14 to 18 of Genesis 1, which say that the sun, moon and stars appeared on the fourth day of creation. Yet verse one of the chapter says, "God created the heaven and the earth" (Genesis 1: 1); not "God created the earth and the heaven!"

There is an easy way to explain this seeming contradiction. Verses 14 to 18 say two things. They say that God *made* the sun and the moon. They also say that He placed or put them in the sky. If He created them before the earth He could still have put them in the sky on the fourth day, and this may be what these verses are really telling us. One way of putting the sun and moon in the sky would have been by the sky becoming clear for the first time. A quite different way would have been to bring the earth into orbit around the sun from somewhere outside the solar system. Both are quite possible explanations.

Some Christians do believe that the earth was created first, all on its own, and that the rest of the universe was not created till the fourth day. If this is true, of course, it means that scientific theories of the universe are wrong. This is not because the science has been done badly, but because all the things described in Genesis chapter one were miracles and so outside of science, i.e. they did not obey scientific laws.

In either case, the Bible makes it clear that by a miracle God created the whole universe out of nothing. As the letter to the

Hebrews says, "Through faith we understand that the worlds were framed by the word of God, so that things which are seen (i.e. the material universe) were not made of things which do appear" (Hebrews 11: 3).

The book of Nehemiah can have the last word: "Thou hast made heaven, the heaven of heavens, with all their host, the earth, and all things that are therein, the seas and all that is therein, and thou preservest them all; and the host of heaven worshippeth thee" (Nehemiah 9: 6).

In these words we can recognise the whole of creation. The sky (the heavens), the universe beyond the sky (the heaven of heavens), the stars (the heavenly host), the earth, the sea, physical life and the scientific laws (preservation) that control them all. More than that, we see creation bowing down before God. This is another way of saying that the creation shows the glory of God, in all His power and wisdom, and that it obeys the laws that He has made.

The six days of creation

In a moment we will be looking at the days of creation one by one. But first we need to answer two questions about the six days.

First, do the six days cover the *whole* creation, including "the beginning", spoken of in verse one of Genesis chapter one? Or does the sentence, "In the beginning God created the heaven and the earth" (Genesis 1: 1), speak of something that happened *before* the six days began? Once again people disagree about the answer. On one hand, a verse in Exodus suggests that the six days must include the whole creation. "In six days the Lord made heaven and earth, the sea and all that in them is, and rested the seventh day" (Exodus 20: 11).

On the other hand, it would seem sensible if the first day *began* with the creation of light on earth, especially since we read, "God called the light Day" (Genesis 1: 5). If this is true, the earth existed (in an empty, shapeless form) before the six days began.

These two ways of understanding the creation story can be made to agree. We can say that the first day includes everything that happened before light was created on earth. This then agrees with Exodus 20: 11. We can then say that the first day lasted much longer than the other six days of creation because, unlike them, *this* day was not measured as the time between a morning and an evening.

So it is possible to interpret the six days so as to allow a long time before the appearance of light on the earth. During this time many things could have taken place in the way that science claims they did. For example, the earth could have taken a very long time to cool down to its formless, empty condition before the next stage of creation took place.

Once again, some Christians prefer to believe that all six days were just as short as an ordinary day is now. Then it would not be possible for the universe to have been formed by the working of scientific law after the "Big Bang". There would not have been enough time for the stars and galaxies to form.

Because God can replace scientific law by miracle at any time He chooses, this interpretation is just as likely to be true. God could have created the universe just as it is now, without using scientific law to bring it from the miracle-of-beginning to its present state. He might have formed the empty earth by His command, already cool and ready for the next act of creation. This is something we must make up our own minds about. Neither interpretation contradicts the view that Genesis is true history.

What about the length of the other five days? We have seen that the first day might have been very long because it did not begin with a morning at all. So it may stretch backwards in time, before light was created on earth. But the other days were different. Each one was the time between one morning and the next. For example we read, "And the evening and the morning were the third day" (Genesis 1: 13). The idea here seems to be that a day began with a morning and that this was followed by an evening and the *next* morning. The day in question thus finished when the next morning began.

Now these days of creation must have been very like our days now. They would have been caused by the earth turning on its axis, just as day and night are caused now. The light, created on the first day, must have come from some star or other distant source. It may even have come from our own sun, if we take the fourth day as the time when the sun was first revealed in the sky rather than the time when it was created.

So it seems that the days of creation (except possibly the first day) were ordinary days and not long periods of time.

There are three ways, however, that the days might have been longer than an ordinary day.

Firstly, the earth may have turned on its axis much more slowly then than it does now. If it turned ten times more slowly, the day would have been ten times as long, and so on. Some of the other planets in our solar system have very long "days".

Secondly, the mornings and evenings may not have been caused by the earth turning on its axis at all, but by a brilliant star flashing on and off. If this is so, the days could have been of any length. This is not very likely because it would be difficult to imagine this happening once the sun had appeared (on the fourth day) to "rule" the day and to "separate the light from the darkness" (see figure 26).

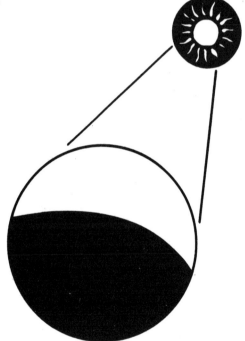

Fig. 26 Day is separated from night on earth by light coming from one direction only.

Thirdly, time itself may have changed since the creation! I know this is hard to imagine but it is not impossible. Since the work of the famous scientist Albert Einstein, the scientific view of time has been quite different from our ordinary ideas. According to Einstein, clocks go faster or slower depending on the speed at which they are moving. For something moving nearly as fast as light itself, time is stretched out, so that things seem to happen very slowly. Also, time can be warped or bent by the force of gravity!

If even science says that time can be changed in these ways, it is clear that time could easily be changed by God's command. Perhaps we are wasting our time arguing about how long were the days of creation. The trouble we have (working out how so much could happen in each of the creation days) may be because we do not understand time itself. Perhaps this was too complicated for God to explain in the Bible, although the New Testament does give us a hint when it says, "One day is with the Lord as a thousand years, and a thousand years as one day" (2 Peter 3: 8).

The first day

Almost all of Genesis chapter one is taken up with things that happened on earth. The rest of the universe is spoken about only in the first verse and on the fourth day of creation. Even on the fourth day, when the sun, moon and stars are put in the sky, the point of view is an earthly one. The chapter is mainly about the earth.

Nothing is said about how God made the earth. We are told that He created it in the beginning and the next thing we read is, "The earth was without form and void; and darkness was upon the face of the deep. And the Spirit of God moved upon the face of the waters" (Genesis 1: 2). To say the earth was "formless" or without shape does not mean it was not round. It almost certainly *was* round (or spherical) as it is today. The verse means that there were no hills and valleys, no continents and seas. It was a sphere with a smooth surface and that surface was water; one great blanket of water over all the earth! There was no light. Everything was pitch black. But God was at work.

The word "spirit" can also mean wind, but always has the first meaning when it is joined with the name of God. So we are told that God Himself, by His Spirit, was still busy with the material world. God's miracle of creation did not finish once He had made the heavens and the earth. Scientific law was now in force (for example, the waters on the earth's surface were kept there by the law of gravity). But at the same time God was moving over those

waters, ready for a new miracle to be performed. "Then God said,
'Let there be light': and there was light" (Genesis 1: 3).

Does this describe the first creation of light, or just the first light
on earth? Either is possible. If the universe was made before the
earth, light probably existed already but had not penetrated the
the darkness of earth (caused by thick cloud?). Remember that
the darkness was "over the surface of the deep". It does not say
that darkness was everywhere in the universe, but only that the
earth was dark.

To say that light had already been created (at the same time as
matter) and that it only broke through to earth in verse 3 does not
make this any less of a miracle. The words "God said" tell us that
this was a new command from God, and so not the work of
natural or scientific law. The breaking-through of light was not
just a natural thinning of the clouds. Something happened that
could not have happened by natural law.

Next we read that God separated the light (day) from the darkness (night). This probably means that half of the earth was lit up
while the other half was dark, exactly as it is now. The line separating day from night moves across the globe as it turns on its axis.
This also means of course that the light must have come from one
direction and that the earth was turning, so that mornings and
evenings followed one another, just as they do now (see figure 26,
page 112).

The second day

Only one thing happened on the second day. A gap was made
between water which stayed on the earth's surface (an ocean) and
water which was high above the earth. This gap was the sky or
heaven.

Can we picture this? One way of understanding it is shown by
figure 27. The first diagram shows what things may have been like
on day one, before light appeared on earth. The waters were not
all liquid, like an ocean, but partly or mostly vapour and cloud.
The cloud layer may have been very thick, stopping any light
from getting through.

At God's command, a lot of the cloud either condensed to water
or else evaporated to become clear vapour, allowing light to shine
on earth for the first time. On the second day some of the vapour
condensed (turned to liquid water), leaving an ocean on the earth's

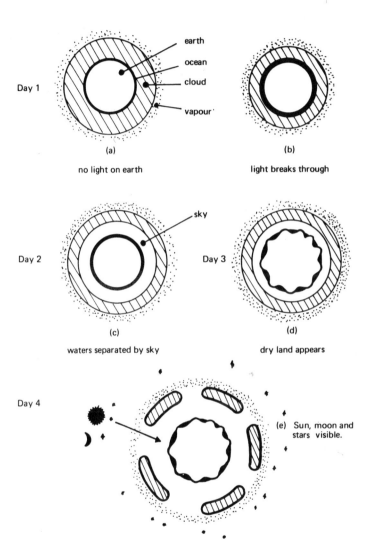

Day 1

(a)

earth
ocean
cloud
vapour

no light on earth

(b)

light breaks through

Day 2

(c)

sky

waters separated by sky

Day 3

(d)

dry land appears

Day 4

(e) Sun, moon and stars visible.

Fig. 27 The earth during the first four days of creation. A possible scheme.

surface together with a layer of vapour and cloud high up in the atmosphere. The cloud in this layer was thin enough to let light through but too thick to let the sun and moon be seen. Below this layer was an open gap, or sky, clear of water vapour as shown in diagram 27c. Genesis chapter two tells us that this all happened without rainfall.

This of course is just one idea of how it might have been. Once again, the separation of the waters was a miracle, because it happened by a new command from God.

The third day

On the third day, dry land appeared for the first time. The liquid water on the surface of the earth was gathered into seas instead of being all over the globe as before.

The dry land could have been made to appear by shrinkage of the earth's core. This would have made the solid crust of the earth wrinkle, just as an apple skin wrinkles as its inside dries out and shrinks. The wrinkled crust would have made the water run into the valleys, leaving the hills sticking up above the water (see figure 27d).

Once again, this is only one possible idea of how it happened. It seems quite a good idea though, because Genesis says the waters were "gathered" into "seas". This suggests the idea of water running into valleys or basins, rather than being lost in some way to make land appear.

It is easy to imagine these things happening by scientific law. For example, the core of the earth would shrink if it cooled down. However, it seems that once again a miracle was involved, perhaps making a natural process happen much more quickly than it would usually do. Once the crust had wrinkled, of course, it did not need a miracle to gather the waters into seas. The natural law of gravity would look after that!

Life appears on earth

We are still looking at the third day. The dry land has appeared. Now the first living things, grass, plants and trees, are created by the command of God. "And God said, Let the earth bring forth grass, the herb yielding seed and the fruit tree yielding fruit after his kind" (Genesis 1: 11).

The first life on earth was plant life. It was created on dry land, not in the sea. From the outset, each "kind" of plant or tree existed separately, i.e. it reproduced only "after its kind". This agrees with our experience now, that living things always reproduce their own kind. There is no hint of any kind of evolution here.

How did God create the plant world? We cannot answer that question scientifically because this was a miraculous act. But it is interesting to notice that the earth brought forth or "sprouted" these plants and trees. That is, they did not appear fully grown in a puff of blue smoke, as in a conjuring trick. They were created *in* the earth in seed form and then developed and grew in the normal way (i.e. as described by scientific law). The miracle probably made atoms and molecules that were already there join together into living molecules and then arranged these molecules into cells and finally seeds. At that point the miracle ended and natural law took over.

The fourth day

The action now moves from earth to the heavens. Remember, though, that the viewpoint is still from earth. It is only because of this that the sun, moon and stars could be said to be placed or put in the sky. "And God said, Let there be lights in the firmament of the heaven to divide the day from the night; and let them be for signs, and for seasons, and for days and years" (Genesis 1: 14).

As I said before, this could mean two things. Either the universe was created after the earth, on the fourth day; or else this verse teaches that the sun, moon and stars became visible (i.e. could be seen) on the fourth day (see figure 27e). I prefer the second explanation because

   (i) the night and day were already separated on the first day, and our verse says that the sun and moon were created to do just this,

  (ii) we are told that God created the "heaven and the earth" not the "earth and the heaven",

 (iii) light was given on the first day, and the light must have come from *something* outside of earth. Part of the universe must have existed to supply this light (light itself is part of the creation). It makes more sense if the whole universe was created in the beginning, not on the fourth day.

Of course, it would not need a miracle to clear the clouds away

so that the sun could be seen. But once again we read the words:
"Then God said . . .", which, we believe, suggest a new command
or miracle from God. This is not difficult to explain. Some important Bible miracles (like the crossing of the Red Sea by the Israel-
ites) are miracles of timing. That is, the cause of what happened
was natural (like the strong wind that drove back the waters of the
Red Sea). But it happened at exactly the right moment. That was
the miracle!

So the clearing of the sky may have been a miracle of timing.
Or, of course, it may have happened in a way that was not possible
by the working of scientific law. In either case it was a true miracle.

The fifth day

The first animal life next appeared in the sea. "And God said,
Let the waters bring forth abundantly the moving creature that
hath life" (Genesis 1: 20). We cannot imagine just how the sea
creatures were created. We do not know if they were created as
eggs or as grown animals. What we are told is that the waters
teemed with life, from the tiniest plankton to the "great sea
monsters". That the seas and rivers were once filled with living
things explains the enormous number of marine fossils and the
great chalk deposits made from the skeletons of tiny sea creatures
(see plate 12).

The fifth day also saw the creation of birds. Along with the
life of the sea, each type of creature was created "after its kind",
i.e. separately. We also read that "God blessed them, saying, Be
fruitful and multiply" (Genesis 1: 22). So God wanted the living
things that He had made to fill the world. Some will wonder how
this could go on and on. Would there be room enough for
them all?

The Bible teaches that when man was created he was made to
live for ever and not to die. For mankind, death came because of
sin. But we are not told that the plant and animal worlds did not
have death. In fact, there must have been "death" of some sort
for the plants and trees to "yield seed". (The flower and the fruit
must both die before the seed is released.) It is quite possible, then,
that animals did die (though not by violence or illness) even before
the sin of Adam. It was man, made in the image of God, who was
so different from the animals that he was immortal.

The sixth day

The rest of the animal kingdom, from insects to cattle, was created on the sixth day. Chapter two of Genesis tells us that "Out of the ground the Lord God formed every beast of the field, and every fowl of the air" (Genesis 2: 19).

Today science helps us to understand this. Living things are made up of exactly the same atoms (carbon, oxygen, hydrogen, sulphur, etc.) that make up the "ground", i.e. the earth, its rocks and its atmosphere. This is an example of how science has made a difficult Bible verse easier to understand. The miracle of creation lies in the way God made those atoms join up into special molecules, like DNA and protein, and the way He wrote the genetic code on them.

If we had been there, what would we have seen? There is no way of telling. But if it helps us to imagine something, this illustration might help.

Have you ever seen a film of, say, a frog's egg hatching out into a tadpole? A fertilised egg is put under a microscope and photographs are taken on a cine film. One photograph is taken every five minutes. The single egg cell divides into two, these two into four, four into eight and so on. As the number of cells grows, some cells start to make different parts of the creature.

This happens slowly. But when the film is shown on a screen at the usual speed of sixteen pictures each second, we see the whole growth of the creature happen in front of our eyes in less than a minute! Perhaps that is rather like what we would have seen if we watched God create the animals. But of course we do not know. We were not there!

The creation of man

On the sixth day also, God created man. The second chapter of Genesis says that as with the animals, "The Lord God formed man of the dust of the ground and breathed into his nostrils the breath of life" (Genesis 2: 7). Yet man was different from the animals. As we saw in the very first chapter of this book, man is made like God Himself. He belongs not only to the material world, but to the spiritual world also.

Chapter two of Genesis tells us that the first woman was made out of one of Adam's ribs or sides. (The Hebrew word is usually translated "side". Nowhere else, except in Genesis chapter two, is it translated "rib".) Science has shown how every living cell has all the information inside it to build the whole creature. So what may seem a difficult story to believe is wholly possible.

Genesis also tells us that man was given charge of the world. He was made to rule over the seas, the sky and the earth and everything in them. Because of sin, says Hebrews chapter two, we do not see man in charge of nature today. Rather, we see ourselves fighting to stay alive in an unfriendly world, threatened by cold, drought, storm and disease as well as by our fellow men.

That is why Jesus Christ came, to cancel out the terrible results of sin and to save those who trust in Him for their forgiveness.

One day, says the Bible, we shall see mankind and nature restored. Those who trust in Jesus Christ will then reign with Him, not only over nature as did Adam, but over the spiritual world too.